LEGAL HANDBOOK
FOR SMALL BUSINESS

LEGAL HANDBOOK FOR SMALL BUSINESS

Marc J. Lane

amacom

A Division of American Management Associations

Library of Congress Cataloging in Publication Data
Lane, Marc J
    Legal handbook for small business.
    Includes index.
    1. Small business—Law and legislation.
I. Title.
KF1659.L36   346'.73'0652   77-13774
ISBN 0-8144-5452-6

© 1977 AMACOM

A division of American Management Associations, New York.
All rights reserved. Printed in the United States of America.

Second Printing

**For my parents,
with love**

PREFACE

This is a game plan. It traces your legal decision making from the earliest stage of business awareness through all the operational challenges you are likely to meet, and it concludes with the yes-and-no factors that lead the small enterprise to its ultimate choice—to go public or not.

Along the way, legal decisions are viewed as the third dimension to business decisions, the dimension that makes them real. The law's requirements are shown to be fully compatible with the best, most practical answers to even the hardest dollars-and-cents business choices.

A word of caution: although this book explores the principal legal opportunities and pitfalls you are apt to encounter as the head of a small business, don't make the mistake of thinking that a book can replace your lawyer. Only he can apply all the nitty-gritty legal specifics to your special situation. Only he can assess the impact of your state's laws (which, because of their diversity, have generally been excluded from our consideration). And only he will know the very latest shifts in the wind's direction out of Washington.

I hope you will find the common-sense approach refreshing. Most legal jargon has been omitted, and the fat-free narratives and meaty checklists that guide your way have been cross-referenced for your ease in research. Surely, you will find this handbook useful as a look-it-up source, but I hope you will find it thoroughly readable and won't put it on the shelf until you've gone from cover to cover.

Acknowledgments

Writing is a collaboration. While I honestly must assume the whole blame for all that follows, I thankfully share any praise . . .

. . . with my wife, Rochelle, and daughters, Allison and Amanda, who saw less of their husband and father than they might have were it not for this effort;

. . . with my secretary, Bee K. Schulman, my paralegal assistant, Blair Doyle, and my typist, Ilene Sangerman, all of whom worked as hard as I did to capture the law's vitality;

. . . and with my clients, whose successes, it is hoped, will lay the foundation for yours.

MARC J. LANE

CONTENTS

A WORD ABOUT LAWYERS

A centuries-old mystique shrouds the legal profession. Astute lawyers bemoan this fact as much as you do. Just the same, too many of them unwittingly intimidate their clients and ultimately profit from their ignorance.

What follows is a call to action. As a client, you've got inalienable rights. Discover them—Chapter 7 reveals them all—and exercise them.

Your first problem is to find the right lawyer. (Chapter 7 will show you how to do that too.) You'll have a lot of questions for him or her, and when you've finished reading this book, you'll have a pretty clear idea of what the critical questions are. You have a right to expect answers that work for you.

You'll earn the respect of your lawyer—who is on your side, after all—and you'll gain that extra insight you need to make your business all it can be.

1
GETTING INTO BUSINESS

Chiefly the mould of a man's fortune is in his own hands.
—Francis Bacon

1•1
WHERE TO BEGIN?

The logic of pedagogy might insist that we begin at the beginning, but let's not. We must assume that you are unalterably committed to becoming a truly successful entrepreneur, and that your independence is a source of deep personal satisfaction. You enjoy responsibility, inspire confidence in those around you, and think in an organized, rational, yet inventive way.

We must assume, too, no matter how experienced you are, that you will seek and follow good advice. Running a business means dealing with complexities beyond the ken of any one individual; even the "mom and pop" enterprise is a team effort today. From the very beginning, you will confer with your lawyer, your accountant, your banker, and your insurance agent or broker. You will rely on a variety of business information clearing houses, including your local Chamber of Commerce, trade associations, colleges and universities, government offices at every level, the Small Business Administration (whose workshops on starting and managing new enterprises consistently earn high praise), the SBA's SCORE (the Service Corps of Retired Executives, eager to give on-site managerial advice and training on a cost-only basis), private experts of every discipline, and, believe it or not, even your competition and would-be competition.

Our final expectation is that you have a feel for the kind of product or service you will want to offer and access to the starting capital your venture will require. Your experience, your education, and your personality will probably have helped predetermine the general nature of the business soon to be yours. The challenge before you is the shaping of that germinal business concept into the best commercial future you can.

1•2
STARTING FROM SCRATCH

At once the trickiest, the riskiest, and perhaps the most rewarding way to get into business is to start your own from the ground up. Caution must be the innovator's watchword: one-third of all new ventures fail or are discontinued in their first year; two-thirds are out of business within five years.

Any new business poses a major risk for its founder, a risk that needs prior control in the form of product research, market analysis, and profit forecasting, all based on a raft of facts it is your job to learn. The most common business types have the advantage of thousands of forebears whose conquests and defeats have lessons to tell. Less traditional products and services dictate more intensive inquiry before an entrepreneurial commitment can be made. At the bare minimum, you and your attorney will want to study these variables:

⇒ *Regulation.* What licensing laws affect your business choice, and can you comply with them? How onerous are applicable consumer protection, environmental, antitrust, and labor laws?

⇒ *Risk.* Apart from the inevitable risk of investment capital, what other risks are forseeable and how easily may they be controlled or insured against?

⇒ *Location.* If the business opportunity before you is tied to a given site, is that site intrinsically destined for profit in its cost/rent and real estate tax structure? In its proximity to the source of your supplies and materials and to your defined market? In the population dynamics and attitudes of its community? In its access to prospective employees? In its competitive advantages? In its zoning? In the services it furnishes and the cost of those services—rail, shipping, police and fire protection, electricity and gas, water, sewage, whatever else you might need?

⇒ *Taxes.* In addition to federal income taxation, can you afford to pay the applicable state and local income taxes? Will your business, especially if capital-intensive, be subject to significant personal property taxes? Can you reasonably bear the burden of sales or occupation taxes? Or, on the other hand, will your jurisdiction foster commercial and industrial development through tax incentives or tax holidays?

⇒ *Capital requirements.* How much will you need to invest before profitability is achieved, months or even years from now? What will your *organizational expenses* be for market surveys and investigations, for projections and estimates, for legal and accounting services through the organization of your business structure? With a view toward maintaining fixed assets at a minimum, what will your *start-up costs* be for initial inventories, equipment and machinery, land and building? Can you estimate your profit margin and first-year sales volume and determine what your *operating expenses* will run until your projected turnaround date, including the cost of replenishing inventories (and taking advantage of prompt-payment discounts), payrolls, and other routine business expenses?

⇒ *Return.* Ultimately, will your business be likely to pay a better-than-savings-account return on your investment plus reasonable compensation for your efforts?

1•3
THE IDEAL PURCHASE

For many, a ground-zero start-up presents an exciting and irresistible challenge. For others, the risks are simply too high. One alternative is the purchase of a going concern. With planning, you might benefit from your predecessor's hard-won knowledge in all these ways:

- ✓ You can by-pass the hassle of refining a fuzzy business idea into a product line, a location, a customer base, inventories, employees, and all the rest.
- ✓ You can inherit the goodwill someone else spent years to build.
- ✓ You can forgo the lean years brand-new businesses invariably struggle through.
- ✓ And, with luck, you can pick up a real bargain, especially if you are buying from someone who needs quick cash or just can't wait to retire.

1•4
YOUR LAWYER'S CHECK-UP

Success is rarely easy and never automatic, even for the prospective purchaser with a blank check. Consistently profitable, trouble-free businesses are seldom sold. (Would you sell one if you owned it?) Be skeptical, and demand strict proof that the venture for sale will form a solid basis for your growth.

Business achievements are the dollars-and-cents product of valuable legal rights. A legally sound enterprise is capable of attaining genuine business success; a legally defective one must be cured at any cost before healthy business growth can commence. For that reason, a critical but objective head-to-toe check-up must be your lawyer's first assignment. The examination he systematically conducts will lay bare the legal reality of the enterprise that interests you. No significant business element should escape his attention:

- ⇒ *Transferability of assets.* See that he scrutinizes documents of title and public records to confirm that the assets for sale are free of encumbrances and restrictions on use.
- ⇒ *Intellectual property.* Trademarks, patents, and copyrights should all be reviewed to assure their legality and scope (Chapter 4).
- ⇒ *Contractual relations.* Rights and obligations under existing contracts, leases, permits, and licenses will all require study.

⇒ *Governmental regulation.* The burden of compliance with current and proposed antitrust, environmental, and consumer protection legislation will need assessment.

⇒ *Employees' rights.* The venture's labor obligations should be examined in light of the Employee Retirement Income Security Act, the Occupational Safety and Health Act, your state's workmen's compensation statute, and other relevant standards. Overall employee benefit commitments should be checked to verify adherence to Treasury and Labor Department pronouncements and to project future costs (Chapter 9).

⇒ *Accounting data.* Your lawyer should rely on an independent analysis by your accountant and integrate his findings into the "legal audit" process. Accounting conclusions—about the age and turnover of inventories, the age, cost, depreciation and insured value of assets, the age and apparent collectibility of accounts receivable, and so much more—will prove invaluable to you in evaluating the true worth of a business (Chapter 3).

⇒ *Securities law compliance.* In the corporate context, shareholdings should be traced to keep you on the safe side of Securities and Exchange Commission regulations and state "Blue Sky" (securities) laws. (See sections 11•8 and 11•9)

1•5
THE TELL-TALE TWENTY

These issues and others worth exploring demand access to legal documentation of virtually every description. Move deliberately, and make no purchase decision until all these documents are made available to you:

1 A list of all states where the seller is incorporated, qualified, or authorized to do business, and the respective inception dates of that authority.
2 Copies of all the seller's patents, trademarks, copyrights, licenses, and any agreements for such rights.
3 All real estate, equipment, and motor vehicle leases to which the seller is a party, whether as lessor or lessee.
4 Deeds to all real estate the seller owns.

5 Titles to all motor vehicles the seller owns.
6 All instruments creating liens, encumbrances or charges against any of the seller's real or personal property.
7 A list of all banks where the seller maintains accounts and safety deposit boxes, the names of all those with access to them, and comprehensive statements of account provided by such banks.
8 A list of all securities the seller owns.
9 A list of all outstanding powers of attorney executed by the seller.
10 A list of all the seller's officers and directors (or, if the business is unincorporated, all top-level employees) and their salaries, bonuses, and benefits in the nature of compensation.
11 All employment contracts.
12 All labor union contracts.
13 All stock bonus, stock option, and retirement plans and their qualification status; any hospitalization, medical reimbursement, and insurance plans.
14 A list of all pensioned employees whose pension benefits are unfunded, whether such pensions have been reduced to a written instrument or not.
15 A list of all employees who will be eligible to retire within the next five years by reason of any formal or informal company plan or policy.
16 A list of any cease-and-desist orders or injunctions in force, any pending litigation, workmen's compensation claims, and discrimination and environmental complaints.
17 Recent profit-and-loss statements and balance sheets, supported by copies of recent federal and state income tax returns and the report of the last Internal Revenue audit.
18 All continuing contracts for the purchase of materials, supplies, and equipment.
19 All contracts and pending bids relating to projects over $10,000 (or a lesser sum for smaller businesses).
20 All contracts continuing over the next year (except minor, routine sales contracts, purchase orders, and supply contracts).

1•6
TO BUY OR NOT TO BUY?

Sit down with your attorney and extract and assimilate the legal data that count. Then translate them into the make-it-or-break-it business considerations that will influence your decision to buy or not to buy. If the following questions yield answers that make you squirm, look elsewhere.

⇒ Why is the business being sold? Are there sound personal reasons, or does a fatal flaw compel a sale?

⇒ What are the prospects for future growth and profit? What is your candid assessment of the location, the market, the product or service, the competition?

⇒ Are the tangible assets worth buying, or have they deteriorated and become obsolete? Does the equipment do its job efficiently, or is it outdated? And is the inventory really valuable, or is it a herd of white elephants?

⇒ Can the intangibles generate a profit for you? What fraction of accounts receivable is worthless? Have the patents, contract rights, or franchises made money in the recent past? If so, are there forseeable circumstances that might change that profitability?

⇒ Can the goodwill really be sold, or is it tied to the personality of the seller? Will he become an employee of yours? Will he sign a noncompetitive agreement? How much ill will offsets the goodwill?

⇒ What liabilities might you unwittingly be assuming? What contingent liabilities can you spot?

⇒ How important are the key employees? Are they happy? Will they remain with the enterprise? Are they replaceable? At what cost?

⇒ What operational changes will you require? What will these improvements cost?

1•7
THE PRICE OF PROFIT

Even if you are satisfied that a business opportunity is ideal, it will only make sense for you at a reasonable price. Rarely will a buyer and a seller agree that an enterprise's *net book value—*

the sum of its tangible assets (at cost less accumulated depreciation) minus its liabilities—is its fair market value. Fancy
appraisals aside, negotiating a purchase price usually takes
the form of old-fashioned horse-trading.

To facilitate bargaining, all kinds of valuation formulas
have been developed. This one does an exceptionally good
job of guesstimating the value of profit-related business
assets:

1   Start with *tangible net worth*—the market value of all cur-
    rent and long-term assets less liabilities.
2   Estimate what you might earn if you invested the
    business's net worth in some other investment of similar
    risk.
3   Add a reasonable salary for an owner-operator of the
    business to arrive at an approximation of the income you
    would earn elsewhere on your investment in time and
    money.
4   Determine the average annual earnings over the last few
    years (before deducting the owner's take) adjusted to re-
    flect current profit trends. Use a pretax figure so that
    more than one business can be valued comparably, with-
    out revision for varying tax brackets.
5   Subtract the sum of the earning power (2) and the reason-
    able salary (3) from the average net profit figure (4)
    and you will compute the excess earning power of the
    business.
6   This excess earning power is multiplied by a "years of
    profit" factor to calculate the fair market value of good-
    will, including all intangibles. The years-of-profit multi-
    plier is selected after considering a number of valuation
    variables, including the uniqueness of the intangibles of-
    fered, the costs of bringing a new concern to the present
    stage of development, and the familiarity of the product
    name. A new but successful venture might call for a one-
    year profit figure; a firm with a long and proud profit
    history might justify a factor of five or more.
7   The purchase price would be the sum of the adjusted

tangible net worth (1) and the value of the intangibles (excess earnings times years-of-profit) (6).

Here is a step-by-step illustration:

(1) Adjusted value of the tangible net worth		$75,000
(2) Earning power (10%)	$ 7,500	
(3) Owner-operator's salary	20,000	
	$27,500	
(4) Average annual net profit, before owner-operator's draw	31,000	
(5) Excess earning power (4) − (2) and (3)	$ 4,000	
(6) Goodwill, applying a 5-year multiplier for a well-established business [5 × (5)]		20,000
(7) Purchase price [(1) + (6)]		$95,000

If the total of the earning power (2) and the reasonable salary (3) were to exceed the enterprise's average annual net profit (4), the seller would not be paid for his goodwill: his business simply would not earn what you, as the buyer, could create through outside investment and effort. In such a situation, you might fix the purchase price by capitalizing the average annual profit, after the owner-operator's draw, by a reasonable rate of return. Assuming a $24,000 average annual net profit in our example, the computation would look like this:

$24,000 net profit (4) − $20,000 draw (3) = $4,000 after-draw profit

$4,000 after-draw profit ÷ .10 rate of return = $40,000 purchase price

Exactly what would you get for your money? You might consider a purchase of corporate stock (to gain the benefit of a net operating loss carry forward, for instance) or a partnership interest (to create a tax shelter), but the hidden liabilities associated with the acquisition of an existing business interest frequently compel the simple purchase of business assets without the assumption of business obligations. It would thus be the business assets—and not a legal entity—that you would buy.

Exhibit A. Purchase price allocation checklist.

Value These Assets Relatively High	*Here's Why*
Supplies	Their cost is deductible as an expense.
Accounts receivable	Bad debts will be deductible for accrual basis taxpayers.
Inventories	A high valuation will reduce your taxable profit.
Patents, copyrights, and other intellectual property with a short remaining life	Their cost can be quickly recovered through amortization.
Tangible assets permitted accelerated depreciation	You can deduct their cost even faster than their value to you diminishes.
Noncompetitive agreement	When contractually severed from goodwill, its cost is deductible ratably over its term.

Value These Assets Relatively Low	*Here's Why*
Long-lived tangible assets, ineligible for accelerated depreciation	If you can't write them off rapidly, they simply are not tax favored.
Land	Never wasting away, it's just not depreciable.
Stocks and bonds	Securities aren't depreciable either.
Goodwill	Its cost is recoverable only when you sell your business.

Your allocation of cost among various assets will have dramatic tax-saving or tax-aggravating consequences, the effective equivalent of paying much less or much more for your business. As a general rule, reasonably slant your purchase price toward assets that would be denied capital gain treatment on disposition. When the seller is granted a tax advantage, the buyer is usually deprived of one. Let Exhibit A be your negotiating checklist.

1•8
PAYMENT POSSIBILITIES

The actual payment of the purchase price need not be C.O.D. Your method of payment should be a creative response to the needs of both buyer and seller. Consider these options:

- ✔ *An installment purchase.* Make a down payment of less than 30 percent of the total purchase price, with the balance evidenced by a note. The seller will qualify for capital gain treatment, and the payments on your note will be spread over a period of years to ease the purchase price burden.
- ✔ *Part purchase, part lease.* Create a tax deduction for your lease payments, and defer much of the seller's taxable gain.
- ✔ *A contingent pay-out.* Pay an agreed sum down, with the balance contingent on future earnings. You will be paying for no more than you actually realize, and you can use the cash in the business to pay off the seller.
- ✔ *A "non-sale."* Take advantage of the seller's brainpower. Keep him on as a partner or a participating consultant. Or issue notes to him for a portion of the purchase price. Your future success will benefit him directly, so you know he will help make your venture profitable.

1•9
PROCEDURAL POINTERS

Once the seller and you agree about the substance of your transaction, both attorneys will proceed to draft a purchase agreement, spelling out your mutual intent in precise detail.

You will notice at least a few safeguards that may never have entered your discussions, but will protect your purchase:

⇒ Your lawyer should demand compliance with your state's Bulk Sales Act, requiring prior notice of your purchase to all your seller's creditors. That way, they will have an opportunity to assert claims against any assets being transferred, and you can take possession without fear of a later challenge to title.
⇒ Closing adjustments should be delimited, along with any other liabilities you might be assuming.
⇒ The seller's noncompetitive agreement should be reasonably defined in time and geographic scope so you can rely on it.
⇒ The seller may warrant his legal compliance, his freedom from pending litigation, the absence of any undisclosed liabilities, the validity of his patents, his sole assumption of risk pending the sale's closing, the accuracy of his last balance sheet, the condition of the equipment you are buying—in short, any fact you need to be sure about before you make your purchase commitment. And the seller's warranties will become an *indemnification,* holding you harmless from any damage you might suffer by reason of his breach of warranty.
⇒ Your down payment may be held *in escrow* by an impartial third party from whom it can be recovered if the seller fails to perform as promised.
⇒ As additional security against an eventual breach, you might have the sale structured so that a part of your purchase price is "held back" until the seller's full performance is satisfactorily completed.

1•10
FRANCHISING: A HAPPY HYBRID?

Franchising is another alternative for the would-be entrepreneur. It is a system of selective distribution which avoids some of the risks of a new business but still gives you the personal satisfaction of initiating your own venture. A franchise is a license to market a product or service in a standardized, systematized way. It is usually granted in exchange for a set fee, an ongoing percentage of the investor's profits, and the investor's agreement to uphold the standards of the trademark that the franchisor, its owner, may impose. The business of franchising has enjoyed a veritable explosion in recent years. Its appeal is obvious:

- *Existing goodwill.* You will be dealing in a proven and well-known product or service. It stands to reason that you should get off to a faster start and significantly reduce the risk of failure.
- *Relatively small capital investment.* The franchisor will have already undertaken substantial steps in research, marketing and advertising and you won't be responsible for most of the costs. What's more, the franchise name might well help you attract financing.
- *Good help from the beginning.* The franchisor may help select your location, negotiate your lease, raise your capital, and supply your equipment and a time-tested design for your physical layout.
- *Continuing managerial expertise.* At best, you will benefit from all the franchisor's experience. You may be offered management assistance, on-site employee training, inventory control aids, accounting help, and more.
- *Mass buying power.* A large franchisor can demand volume discounts and pass them along to you.
- *Wide-area promotion.* The impact of the franchisor's advertising program may do more for a small businessman than he could ever afford to do for himself.

1•11
LOSING CONTROL

The advantages of protection and guidance carry with them the big disadvantage of the franchisor's control over the investor. Even the most reputable franchise opportunity suffers from these restrictions:

- x *You will not really be your own boss.* A franchise will be your investment but not your creation. Any franchisor will impose standards and controls which will greatly limit your free will, even your ability to branch out into other lines or to sell your franchise!

x *You will share your profits.* After you pay your initial franchise fee, you will be required to pay the franchisor a percentage royalty—forever.

x *Your financial security will be at the mercy of the franchisor.* Your franchise agreement will probably give the franchisor the right to define territories, settle interfranchise disputes, set sales quotas, and terminate your contract.

1•12
EVALUATING THE FRANCHISE OFFER

The first step in relating a franchise opportunity's pros and cons to your unique requirements is a comprehensive evaluation of the franchise offer. With the recent history of fraudulent "pyramid" promotions, the franchise investor should be asking pointed questions without hesitation. After studying *Franchise Company Data* (available free from Sales and Distribution, U.S. Department of Commerce, Washington, D.C. 20230) and whatever relevant information you can muster from the National Association of Franchised Businessmen (1404 New York Avenue, N.W., Washington, D.C. 20005) launch a tough and thorough investigation:

⇒ *Who is the franchisor?* What is his reputation with his franchisees and the public in general? How long has he been in the business? What is his credit rating? What is his franchise failure rate?

⇒ *What is the product or service?* Is it well known? Is it competitive? Is it something to be genuinely enthusiastic about? Will the need for it endure? Is it unquestionably legal?

⇒ *Where is the market?* What territory would you get and would it be exclusive? Is it adequate? Does it have good growth potential? What competition exists and what looms ahead?

⇒ *Who's got what rights?* Are fees and royalties reasonable? What is your total investment and what do you get for it? What help will the franchisor give you with raising capital, locating, training, and management? Will you be furnished patent and liability insurance? Would you be permitted to sell the franchise? Would you be obligated to carry any new product, or could you opt against one you didn't believe in? Would you have the right to renew your contract, or terminate it for good cause? Has the franchisor complied with all state and federal laws? Would you be obligated to buy specific volumes of inventory, and can inventory be returned for credit? Is there a sales quota? If so, what is the consequence of failing to meet it? Would you be required to contribute to an advertising fund? If so, is the amount reasonable and would you benefit in proportion to your contribution?

⇒ *What will the effect be on you?* How much money are you likely to earn? Would you be better off than you would starting a business on your own? Do the advantages clearly outweigh the disadvantages? Can you comfortably comply with the franchisor's standards?

1•13
A LEGAL LOOK AT THE FRANCHISE AGREEMENT

Once you have completed your preliminary evaluation of the franchise offer, have your lawyer dissect the franchise agreement. He will assess the legality of the instrument as a whole and ascertain the obligations, risks, rights, and liabilities that would be yours. Watch out for these frequently litigated points of potential dispute:

⇒ *The degree of control.* The franchisor's legal right to control derives from the Lanham Act, which makes it his duty to "police the trademark" and insure that product quality and uniformity are maintained. The problem is in defining just how much control is reasonably necessary to police the mark. Too much regulation may be in violation of antitrust laws.

⇒ *The true cost of the franchise.* Most agreements will specify a one-time initial fee plus a royalty on a continuing basis. Be sure these are reasonable, particularly if a minimum royalty is established; and note hidden costs, including minimum maintenance standards, advertising contributions, and insurance.

⇒ *Pricing.* While a franchisor may suggest prices, he is prohibited from instituting price controls.

⇒ *The sources of supply.* The agreement may call for *exclusive dealing,* requiring the franchisee to purchase his supplies from the franchisor or another designated source. But the franchisee may not be forced to buy items he doesn't want, nor may the franchisor *tie,* or condition, his sale of one item on your purchase of another unless both products are clearly necessary to protect the quality of the franchise trademark. In general, you should be free to shop for the best products and prices available.

⇒ *Advertising.* See that any required contributions to an advertising budget are reasonable and not automatically subject to increases. If you can, reserve some authority in fixing the amount and content of local advertising, and satisfy yourself that contractual advertising policies are aimed at benefiting you.

⇒ *Standards and supervision.* Make sure you can live with the requirements. In particular, check the inspection, maintenance, bookkeeping, supervision, and hiring-and-firing provisions. Understand the penalties for violating them.

⇒ *The territory.* Be satisfied that the agreement offers you adequate protection against the franchisor's setting up another location too close for comfort. The franchisor may legally restrict himself by protecting your territory, but he may not place restrictions on your legal right to deal noncompetitively anywhere.

⇒ *Terminations and nonrenewals.* Sales quotas must be reasonable in view of the size, location, and protection of your territory; and they may not be arbitrarily imposed to deprive you of your franchise. The franchisor's right to terminate or nonrenew your agreement should be conditioned on good cause, and should be linked to an equitable repurchase procedure. Yet, you deserve both reasonable renewal rights and the right to terminate your agreement with notice; and your interest needs to be protected in the event of your death or disability.

1•14
A PERSPECTIVE

The major choices are now before you—whether to create a new enterprise, buy an existing one, or operate as the licensee of a parent franchisor. Whichever fits your future, you have already started to recognize that legal decisions and business decisions are inextricably intermeshed. Indeed, one forms the conceptual foundation of the other; and, through your diligence, both will form the foundation of your entrepreneurial success.

2

STRUCTURING
THE ENTERPRISE

Quick decisions are unsafe decisions.
—Sophocles

2 • 1
FOLLOWING THE FORM

Even before you open your doors, you will be wise to select a business unit—a proprietorship, a general partnership, a corporation, or something else. Sometimes the choice of business form is dictated by external factors: high exposure to legal risks, for instance, may suggest the corporate form with its insulation from personal liability; a tax-sheltering objective may force a limited partnership. Other times, the business unit is freely selected by a savvy entrepreneur who is acutely sensitive to the legal, tax, and operational results of his decision.

Whatever prompts your selection, know its consequences. And make the most of your choice by maximizing its strengths and mitigating its weaknesses.

2 • 2
GOING IT ALONE

A *sole proprietor* is simply a person who independently conducts an unincorporated business for profit. The proprietorship is created at will without legal documentation. For this reason alone, it is clearly the easiest and cheapest way to start and run a business, and it may be the best way for you to get started. Ordinarily, all one needs to begin operating as a sole proprietor is compliance with local assumed-name and licensing statutes. Since the enterprise has no legal identity apart from its owner, centralized management can be absolute. There are no directors, no officers, and, indeed, no co-owners to impede free-swinging decision making.

Sometimes the price of all this independence can be surprisingly high. Have your attorney help you assess these hidden costs:

x   A proprietorship leaves you exposed to unlimited personal liability. The business is your alter ego, and judgments entered against it are yours to pay. Of course, you can insure yourself against a multitude of hazards, but some risks are wholly uninsurable and liability for debts is boundless.

x   Since a proprietorship is nothing more than its owner, it dies with him, leaving its assets less its liabilities to his heirs. The prospect of the owner's death or incapacity can cloud dealings with would-be creditors, customers, and employees.

x   Proprietors cannot take advantage of many of the deductible "fringes" enjoyed by corporate shareholder-employees, including sick-pay plans, medical, dental, and hospitalization plans, medical reimbursement plans, group term life insurance, and more. (See sections 10•6 and 10•8)

x   In general, tax planning opportunities are minimal. Inasmuch as the law does not recognize a proprietorship as a distinct entity, the proprietor is taxed on his total business income, whether or not that income is drawn upon for personal use. And taxed income may neither be shifted by using fiscal years, nor controlled by engineering compensation to the owner. Moreover, a parade of tax deductions are lost to the proprietorship, including the amortization of organizational expenses and the business deduction of charitable donations, both of which can create savings for the corporation.

2 • 3
TEAMING UP

The *general partnership* may offer you greater latitude in business planning. An association of two or more persons to conduct a business for profit as co-owners, the partnership is a legally recognized entity. As such, it offers its owners flexibility in sharing operating responsibilities and decision-making authority. Where partners neglect to negotiate and resolve these issues in front, the Uniform Partnership Act will presume equality in both rights and obligations.

The partnership offers great tax opportunities to the investor. The business is a tax reporter, but not a taxpayer. Every year it files an informational return with the Internal Revenue Service, spelling out each partner's proportionate share of profits, gains, losses, deductions, and credits. Each partner then treats these items as if they were realized or incurred by him directly. The big tax advantage is the partnership's limited ability to allocate income-and-expense items among the owners to achieve the best overall tax result.

In negotiating allocations, note that a partner's share of income is taxed to him even if he does not receive it. Any income retained by the partnership merely increases a partner's tax basis in his partnership interest, reducing his taxable gain upon its ultimate sale. A partner's share of losses (including capital losses) is personally deductible, but he may not deduct more than the *adjusted basis* (before reduction by the current year's losses) of his partnership interest at the end of the partnership year in which the loss is incurred. This adjusted basis is the capital contribution, or the original purchase price, of the partnership interest (less any withdrawals) plus accumulated taxed earnings that have not been withdrawn.

Another tax plus is the partner's privilege to deal with the enterprise as a separate legal entity. He can lease or sell property or loan money to the partnership, all with rather controllable tax consequences.

Even with all these benefits, the general partnership is subject to criticism:

x Like the proprietor, the partner is open to unlimited personal liability and, still worse, is liable for the business acts and omissions of his co-partners.

x Any partner can contractually bind the enterprise, since each is its agent. Without a clear-cut agreement, lines of authority can blur; and management by committee can swiftly become no management at all.

x By definition, a partnership is technically dissolved at the death or withdrawal of any partner. A new partner can be admitted only with the consent of all the existing partners. Lacking both continuity of life and free transferability of interests, a partnership often looks fragile to potential backers and employees.

2•4
SOME PARTNERSHIP VARIANTS

To mitigate these defects, new partnership forms have evolved in recent years:

↗ *The joint venture* is simply a short-term general partnership created for a limited purpose. Since the venture ends at the conclusion of a specific project, issues of continuity of life and free transferability become moot.

↗ *The limited partnership* is frequently selected for real estate tax shelters. One or more general partners manage the business and remain personally liable for its debts. The other partners are limited in liability to the extent of their investments. They have no rights in management and may transfer their interests (as provided by contract) without dissolving the partnership. Within legal limits, the lion's share of deductible partnership losses are allocated to the limited partners, who use them to offset taxable income from other sources.

↗ *The real estate investment trust* is an unincorporated trust or association. It is managed by a trustee for the benefit of 100 or more beneficiaries who currently receive at least 90 percent of the trust's income and who individually pay a

tax on that income. REITs, which saw their heyday in the
early 1970s, enjoy the corporate virtues of continuity of
life, free transferability of interests, and centralized management.

↙ *The family partnership* is a common device for splitting income among family members to avoid high tax brackets.
A high-bracket taxpayer gives a partnership interest in his
business, if capital (and not service) is a material income-
producing factor, and pays the applicable gift tax. Future
income is allocated between the donor (entrepreneur) and
donee (family member), allowing reasonable compensation for services rendered to the partnership by the donor,
and a lower overall tax liability is achieved.

2 • 5
COMING TO TERMS

The partnership relationship is complex. Don't back away
from the controversies that will invariably arise. Instead, opt
for candor. Seek out the hot issues and, with your lawyer,
bargain for your best position—*before you get into business.* You
will have gained all that is rightfully yours, with honor and
without the pain of friction among partners. These issues are
worth resolving and reducing to contract form:

⇒ *The partnership's name.* Your lawyer will tell you about the
legal restrictions that limit your choice and will help you
steer clear of any name that's deceptively similar to that of
an existing business.

⇒ *The nature of the business.* Avoid any conflict in entrepreneurial goals. Since a general partnership obligates you
for the business acts and omissions of your co-partners, it
is wise to limit the scope of your business activities by
contract.

⇒ *The duration of the partnership.* A partnership can end on a
predetermined date or it can last indefinitely. Either way,
a partner might withdraw from the enterprise at any time,
without notice, and even in violation of contract, giving
rise to his co-partners' suit for damages. Since damages

may be difficult to value, specify a fair *liquidated damages* amount, to which you would be entitled upon a partner's premature exit.

⇒ *Contributions.* Decide who will contribute what, and when. You may allocate the income from the partnership's eventual sale of a contributed asset to compensate for any difference between its tax basis to the partnership (carried over from the contributing partner) and its fair market value at the time of contribution. Such an arrangement avoids favoring partners who contribute appreciated property.

⇒ *Sales, loans, and leases.* To avoid disparities between tax basis and fair market value, you—or any of the partners—can sell your assets to the partnership at their fair market value and individually realize taxable gains and losses. Or you can lend money to the partnership, which can then buy equivalent assets elsewhere; you will realize interest income on your money, deductible by the partnership. A third option: Consider leasing property to your partnership; the partnership can deduct its payments, and your lease income can be more or less offset by deductible depreciation.

⇒ *Distributions and withdrawals.* Unless you agree otherwise, no partner will be entitled to a guaranteed salary from the partnership. Each will be taxed solely on his allocable share of profits less his allocable share of losses, whether or not the difference is actually distributed to him. Spell out the profit-and-loss split in detail, as well as any rights to distributions. Beyond living expenses and personal tax liabilities, you may want to limit both income distributions and capital withdrawals and let the partnership use its money to grow.

⇒ *Partners' rights and duties.* Remember that you are legally liable for the acts of the partnership. You have a right to know what the partnership is doing, and you have an obligation to fulfill your decision-making responsibilities. Carefully delineate managerial responsibilities, and set up a settlement procedure to resolve conflicts in judgment.

⇒ *Dissolution.* Set out notice requirements for dissolving the partnership and procedures for winding up its business. The partners should agree about the distribution of assets and the payment of liabilities upon dissolution.

⇒ *Continuity.* The admission of new partners requires the consent of all existing partners. Agree on consent mechanics and, more important, agree on a "Buy-Sell" approach. A Buy-Sell agreement can be a near-perfect answer to the structuring problems arising out of a partner's death. The surviving partners are assured of the right to buy his interest, generally with life insurance proceeds, and they retain control of management. The decedent's estate is assured of a fair price (computed by formula), one that will hold up for federal estate-tax purposes.

2•6
WHY INCORPORATE?

A *corporation* is the only business structure that is legally recognized as an artificial person. The law's view that a corporation is an entity separate and apart from its owners inescapably leads to the conclusion that it is liable for its own debts and taxes. As we shall see, this simple thesis reaps special benefits:

↙ *Insulation from personal liability.* A sole proprietor is liable for all his business debts, and a general partner is responsible for the claims of business creditors when partnership assets cannot render full payment, but a corporate stockholder's liability is limited to his investment. And, although shareholders are often called upon to pledge their personal credit in borrowing business funds, trade creditors and employees with wage claims are foreclosed from reaching investors' assets. Moreover, shareholders are usually shielded from all business tort liability.

↙ *Favorable tax treatment.* The corporate federal income tax rates are typically lower than the individual rates for a proprietor or partner. At this writing, the first $25,000 of corporate income is taxed at 20 percent, the next

$25,000 at 22 percent, and the balance at 48 percent. This tax applies after all deductible expenses are subtracted from income, including (1) reasonable compensation to you and other employees, (2) 85 percent of dividends received from domestic corporations, (3) certain bad debts, (4) net operating loss carryforwards, (5) charitable contributions to the extent of 5 percent of taxable income, (6) amortized organizational expenses (over 60 months), (7) and all kinds of fringe benefits for you and your co-workers—workmen's compensation, group term life insurance, death benefits, tax-free reimbursement of medical expenses, and more. Profits not distributed to shareholders—up to $150,000 or even more —can be accumulated in the corporation and can earn passive investment income, which will probably be taxed only at the low corporate rates.

✔ *Continuity of business life.* When a proprietor dies, his business may die with him. When a partner dies or withdraws from a partnership, its business is disrupted and endangered. Yet a corporation may be perpetual, despite the death of an owner or his sale of shares. That stability alone can be enough to keep employees feeling secure and creditors calm. What's more, the corporation offers its owners the greatest range of estate planning possibilities.

✔ *Centralized management.* All general partners have an equal voice in decision making, and each is bound by the business acts of the others. A corporation's shareholders, on the other hand, appoint *directors* to set basic company policy; the directors, in turn, effect that policy through the *officers* they appoint. In small corporations, shareholders, directors, and officers may be the same people. In larger corporations, officers and those they supervise may be structured into their own bureaucracies, or into freewheeling task forces overlapping organizational lines to solve short-term problems. Simple or complex, the corporation is a decision-making form noteworthy for its systematic delegation of legal responsibilities. One result that's important to you is that liabilities will not ordinarily flow through to the owners.

    ✔ *Free transferability of interests.* The sale of a partnership interest will not assure the purchaser's admission to the firm on equal footing with his predecessors; a change in membership requires their prior approval. To convey his interest to a newcomer, a corporate investor needs only to sell his shares and deliver the certificates that represent them. He needn't undermine the business nor compel its dissolution.

    But anticipate some problems: the securities laws may severely restrict transferability. And, even if you are legally able to sell your interest, don't count on a ready market for it. Should you want out, your co-shareholders are likely purchasers. Agree in advance about the terms of any eventual buy-out and you'll be sure to receive a fair price.

    Where it exists, free transferability is a detriment as often as it's a benefit. If your business is heavily dependent on the rapport the principals have developed, consider a contract to restrict transfers to outsiders.

2•7
STEP-BY-STEP INCORPORATION

The advantages may be impressive, but what does it really take to incorporate? The corporate game is one of formalities, and all of them are meaningful. If your situation justifies the time and expense, your lawyer will guide you through these steps:

    ⇒ *Execute some contracts.* You and your fellow investors will sign a comprehensive *subscription agreement,* setting out the purpose and structure of the new corporation, your agreement to contribute assets and their value, and the proposed distribution of corporate stock and notes. You'll also sign *employment agreements,* detailing the duties and rights of shareholder-employees, including their compensation. In addition, you will probably sign a *Buy-Sell agreement* restricting the sale of shares to outsiders and obligating the corporation or its shareholders to buy the stock of a deceased shareholder on the basis of a pre-scribed formula, typically with life insurance proceeds.

⇒ *Pick a state.* Normally the state in which you will operate is the state in which to incorporate. If you contemplate in-terstate activities or a fancy debt-and-equity mix, you might consider Delaware. Exhibit B will tell you why.

Exhibit B

Why They Pick Delaware

Ten Good Reasons

1. There is no corporate income tax in Delaware for companies doing no business there, no tax on shares held by nonresidents, and no inheritance tax on nonresident holders.
2. The private property of shareholders is protected from liability for corporate debts (shareholders' liability is limited to their stock investment), and officers and directors may be indemnified.
3. Stockholders and directors may meet outside Delaware and keep corporate books and records outside the state.
4. Only one incorporator is required, and that incorporator may itself be a corporation.
5. A Delaware corporation may be perpetual and can operate through voting trusts and stockholder voting agreements.
6. Directors may make and alter by-laws and may act by unanimous written consent in lieu of formal meetings.
7. Delaware has no minimum capital requirements. A corporation may issue shares—common and preferred, even in serial classes —without par value, fully paid and non-assessable, for con-sideration or at a price fixed by the directors. And the directors' judgment about the value of property or services is conclusive. They may determine what portion of the consideration received goes to capital, what part to surplus.
8. A Delaware corporation can hold the securities of other cor-porations and all kinds of other property, both in Delaware and outside the state, without limit. It can also purchase its own stock and hold, sell, or transfer it.
9. Any different kinds of business can be conducted in combination.
10. Dividends can be paid out of profits as well as out of surplus.

⇒ *Request IRS rulings on any questionable tax aspects of your incorporation.* Especially in the incorporation of an existing business, it may be a good idea to seek a Treasury Department opinion of your transaction before it's consummated. The Internal Revenue Code's philosophy is to recognize no taxable event in the incorporation of a going concern when incorporators transfer their business assets to the new corporation, receive stock or securities in exchange, and retain control, but be safe.

⇒ *Draft the charter*—the *Articles of Incorporation.* Once filed, they will become the corporation's governing instrument.

⇒ *Hold a shareholders' meeting at once and at least annually thereafter.* The first meeting will see the directors elected.

⇒ *Hold the first directors' meeting* to elect officers, to adopt the bylaws (the rules of internal management), and to approve the corporate seal, the stock certificates (and their issuance), the transfer of property, and the opening of the corporate bank account. The directors will conduct the affairs of the corporation at frequently held meetings. Both shareholders' and directors' meetings should be recorded by minutes, or you'll be hard-pressed to prove they ever happened.

⇒ *Issue stock.* The directors have ok'd the corporation's issuance of stock as provided in the subscription agreement. The actual sale or distribution of corporate stock is regulated by both the states and the federal government. Most initial issues will qualify for an exemption from registration (See sections 11•8 and 11•9). Be sure yours does. In any case, the twin principles of fair dealing and full disclosure must characterize your sale.

When issuing stock, consider an election under Section 1244 of the Internal Revenue Code. If your corporation's total equity capital does not exceed $1,000,000, and if the total amount your corporation receives for stock—either as a contribution to capital or as paid-in surplus—does not exceed $500,000, you are eligible. A written plan indicating the maximum dollar amount of stock to be issued and stating the issuance period (no more than two years) can be adopted by the directors. Losses due to the worthlessness or sale of stock by the shareholders will be treated as ordinary tax-deductible losses, up to $25,000 on a separate return, $50,000 on a joint return.

⇒ *Order a corporate taxpayer ID number* from the IRS and file consents at once, if you are electing Subchapter S status.

2 • 8
SUBCHAPTER S: THE BEST OF TWO WORLDS?

Subchapter S of the Internal Revenue Code allows certain small corporations to be taxed much as partnerships are, allowing them to enjoy the advantages of the corporate form without incurring income tax liability at the corporate level. During its early, lean years, a corporation may make the Subchapter S election, permitting business losses to flow through to its owners and, at the same time, preserving the benefits of corporateness. These are the requirements:

1   At the outset, the corporation must have no more than 10 shareholders. After the first 5 years, it may have as many as 15. Even during the first 5 years, the number may increase to 15 if by inheritance. (A husband and wife are considered one shareholder if their stock is held jointly.)
2   Individuals, estates, or certain types of trusts must own all the stock.
3   Citizens or resident aliens must own all the stock.
4   It must be a domestic corporation and not a member of an affiliated group eligible to file a consolidated tax return.
5   The corporation must have only one class of stock.
6   Its gross receipts must not exceed 80 percent from sources outside the United States or 20 percent from passive investment income (except during the first two taxable years if passive income is less than $3,000).

2 • 9
THE SUB S PLUSES

Subchapter S is not for everyone, but if the foregoing tests are met, the corporate tax advantages may be yours, even while items of income, deduction, and credit pass through to you as an owner. Arrange a meeting with your lawyer and exchange these ideas:

✔ *An adopted tax year.* A partnership's taxable year must coincide with the taxable year of its principal partners. As a result, partners are not able to postpone the recognition of income and loss until a future year. A Subchapter S corporation, like any corporation, can adopt a fiscal year, even if all its shareholders report their taxable income on a calendar-year basis. (See section 3 • 3). Consider the opportunities for acceleration and deferral.

✔ *Fringe benefits.* A partner is not an employee for tax purposes and is not eligible for the fringes that corporate owner-employees, including Subchapter S owner-employees, enjoy. (See section 10 • 6).

✔ *Loss flow-throughs.* The amount of partnership loss a partner may personally deduct is generally limited to the cost of his partnership interest plus his prorata share of partnership liabilities. His loans to the partnership increase the partner's basis for absorbing losses only by his share of the liability. In contrast, a Subchapter S shareholder may deduct his share of the corporate net operating loss up to the cost of his stock plus any corporate debt to him. Therefore any valid loan from the shareholder to the business directly increases his tax basis for absorbing losses.

✔ *Income recognition.* A partner must report his share of partnership income and losses. If a partnership interest is sold before the year's end, the purchaser earns taxable income from the time of the transfer. A Subchapter S corporation's distributions, however, are taxed as dividends (ineligible for the $100 exclusion) in the year the shareholder receives them. Any taxable income remaining in the corporation is taxed to the shareholder in his tax year within the corporation's tax year (or with which the corporation's tax-year ends). Such "undistributed taxable income" is shared by those stockholders who own stock on the last day of the corporation's tax year, so Subchapter S shareholders can redistribute income among themselves or to new owners through the use of good-faith year-end stock transfers.

✔ *Maxi-tax.* Partnership income is so-called "personal service income," taxed at no more than 50 percent. If both capital and services produce substantial income for the partnership, a partner's earned income cannot exceed his share of 30 percent of partnership net profits. Contrast that treatment with Subchapter S shareholder earnings: Dividends are ineligible for the 50 percent maximum-tax ceiling, but all the reasonable compensation paid to a Subchapter S shareholder-employee is eligible.

2•10
PUTTING IT ALL TOGETHER

It should be obvious that your choice of business structure must not be a legal decision by default. Temper overcautious legal thinking with goal-directed business thinking. Insist that your lawyer appreciate your entrepreneurial objectives and that he pragmatically relate them, in detail and in depth, to the law's newest quirks.

3

TALLYING
YOUR PROFITS

Good order is the foundation of all good things.
—Edmund Burke

3•1
SETTING GOALS

The orderly recordation, summarization, and analysis of your enterprise's financial data will tell you where your business is prospering, where it is not, and why. No wonder the tailoring of an accounting system to suit your special needs is a prerequisite to controlled business growth. In defining your accounting objectives, consider this advice:

⇒ Choose your accountant with care and give him your trust. (See section 7 • 8). Whether you retain an independent CPA or hire your own controller, make sure he thoroughly understands your business and its policies. An accountant cannot be expected to develop or implement the best system for you without this basic appreciation of who you are and what you are trying to do. Once the two of you have established rapport, level with him: he cannot be legally responsible for any erroneous business impressions you may have given him.

⇒ Don't overkill. All accounting work must generate information of special value to someone—you and your co-owners, the IRS, or your creditors. Any report or subsystem failing to meet that acid test should be dropped pronto.

No record is eternally valuable to anyone. From time to time, purge what no longer serves a purpose, and you'll gain surer access to the reports you still find meaningful. Exhibit C is a good throw-it-out-already checklist.

⇒ Demand that your system become an integrated whole; a good accounting system is internally consistent.

⇒ Strive for realism. A system that fails to mirror your enterprise's true financial state is valueless. What's more, it will not fulfill your disclosure responsibilities to those with a legal stake in your growth.

⇒ Establish controls. Assure reliability through a sensible network of in-house checks and balances. And periodically bring in *outside* auditors for a truly objective survey.

⇒ Make your system work for you. Put everything you learn to work, and buy only the expertise you intend to use.

3 • 2
FINANCIAL ACCOUNTING vs TAX ACCOUNTING

Understand from the beginning that your accounting system should be functionally responsive. Pure business decisions will be rendered on the basis of the economic conclusions your *financial accounting* subsystem generates. Pure tax decisions will be made only after reviewing information colored by tax notions and derived from your *tax accounting* subsystem. Mixed business-and-tax decisions, as many if not most will be, will require study from both perspectives.

The Internal Revenue Service recognizes the desirability of maintaining two inconsistent sets of data. When reviewing your accountant's reports, learn whether he is submitting a financial officer's report or a tax-slanted, but equally legitimate, tax accountant's report. Here are a few of the differences:

⇒ Some real income, such as interest on municipal bonds, is altogether excluded from tax calculations.

⇒ Some deductions, including bad debts and casualty losses,

Exhibit C. A record-retention checklist.

GENERAL AND FINANCIAL

Capital stock records	Permanent
Bond records	Permanent
Corporate records and minutes	Permanent
Titles and mortgages	Permanent
Expired contracts and agreements	7 years
Year-end general ledgers and trial balances	Permanent
Records of canceled securities	7 years
Insurance records	
Fidelity bonds	3 years
Inspectors' reports	Permanent
Schedules and claims	7 years
Expired fire, liability, auto, and other policies	Optional
Record of policies in force	3 years
Federal and state tax records and returns	Permanent
Records of fixed assets and appraisals	Permanent
Accountants' audit reports	Permanent

SALES AND RECEIVABLES

Accounts receivable ledgers	7 years
Accounts receivable trial balances	3 years
Sales journals	7 years
Copies of invoices	3 years
Ratings and investigations of customers	3 years
Uncollectible accounts files including authorizations for write-off	7 years
Expired contracts with customers	7 years
Records relating to sales to affiliated companies	7 years
Canceled notes receivable and trial balances	7 years
Shipping tickets	3 years

PAYROLLS

Payroll journals and summaries	7 years
Receipted pay checks and time cards	7 years
Payroll deductions records	7 years
Assignments, attachments, and garnishments	3 years
Individual earnings records	Permanent
W-2 forms	3 years
W-4 forms	Permanent

CASH AND COLLECTIONS

Cash receipts and disbursements	Permanent
Bank deposit slips	1 year
Deposit books and stubs	7 years
Bank reconcilement papers	1 year
Records of outstanding checks	7 years
Periodic cash reports	3 years
Canceled checks	Permanent
Canceled payroll checks .	7 years
Bank statements (after audit)	7 years
Petty cash vouchers	3 years

INVENTORIES

General inventory with adjustment records	Permanent
Material ledgers (Perpetual inventory records)	Permanent
Stores requisitions	3 years
Physical inventory records	3 years

PURCHASES AND PAYABLES

Accounts payable ledgers	7 years
Accounts payable trial balances	3 years
Voucher registers or purchase journals	Permanent
Paid bills and vouchers	7 years
Copies of purchase orders	3 years
Bids and offers	7 years
Price records of purchases	Permanent
Purchase contracts	7 years
Bills of lading	3 years

MISCELLANY

Correspondence	
Legal and important matters	Permanent
General	1–5 years
Interim financial statements	Permanent
Social Security returns	Permanent
State sales tax	Permanent
Federal excise tax	Permanent
Monthly trial balances	5 years
Equipment records	Permanent
Expired leases	7 years

may be subject to greater restrictions under tax accounting concepts.

⇒ Some income—particularly prepaid income—and some
deductions—such as "bonus" depreciation (section
3 • 7)—may be reported in different years or in different
ways under the two subsystems.

⇒ Some special tax deductions—among them the *percentage
depletion allowance,* by which the owner of a mine may
recover the cost of a mineral deposit during the period in
which the mineral is extracted—may not represent true
cost deductions for financial accounting purposes.

⇒ The tax provisions for net operating loss carrybacks and
carryforwards will produce widely diverse results between
the two subsystems.

⇒ More and more accountants insist that financial statements should be adjusted for the effects of inflation. Some
subscribe to a "purchasing power" approach, adjusting all
nonmonetary items, including inventories, by an inflation
index. Others record assets (and even liabilities) at market
prices or replacement value.

3 • 3
STARTING THE YEAR OFF RIGHT

A prime function of tax accounting is the computation of
taxable income over a fixed period, usually twelve months,
known as a *taxable year.* The selection of your taxable year is a
surprisingly important decision. With proper timing, income
and expense items can be accelerated or deferred to engineer
favorable tax and cash-flow consequences. Yet, the law requires that your accounting system and the year in which it
operates accurately reflect your business profit profile without
distortion. After a year has been selected, a change is not
easily accomplished, so make your decision deliberately. Here
are your taxable year choices:

1   *The calendar year.* January 1 through December 31 is the
natural choice of most small-business owners, but it is not
always the wisest choice. Should you fail to maintain

adequate accounting records, the calendar year will automatically be elected for you.

2 *A fiscal year.* Choose any twelve-month period ending on the last day of a month other than December. Split your peak season between two taxable years to balance your tax burden. A new corporation can end its initial taxable year in less than twelve months to defer income and postpone the payment of taxes until the business has survived its first critical year.

3 *A 52–53 week year.* By this variant of the fiscal year, you may use an annual accounting period of 52 or 53 weeks, always ending on the same day of the week. Businesses with weekly income cycles might find the 52–53 week year most appropriate.

3 • 4
TIMING YOUR DEBITS AND CREDITS

Once your time frame has been determined, the choice of an accounting method is the biggest accounting decision before you. Any method that's regularly employed in the keeping of your books is permissible, provided it clearly reflects your income. A taxpayer ordinarily cannot change his method of accounting as a matter of right, so give your selection due consideration at the outset. In practice, these methods are most common:

1 The *cash method* records income when it is "constructively" received (that is, available for your use) and deducts expenses when they are paid, unless their deduction at some other time (as in the case of prepaid expenses) would more accurately reflect income. The cash method has the advantage of simple bookkeeping requirements. What's more, it offers the taxpayer an opportunity to defer the receipt of income, to accelerate the payment of expenses, and thus to reduce taxable profit at year-end.

2 The *accrual method* records income when all preconditions to your right to receive it have taken place, even if the money is not yet in your hands. Expenses accrue when

their amounts are reasonably certain and you become liable to pay them. The accrual method realistically matches income and expense items with business events as they occur.

3 Various hybrid methods combine elements of both the cash and accrual methods. All businesses with inventories must use the accrual method to record purchases and sales, but may report other transactions on a cash basis. A taxpayer who is involved in more than one activity may adopt the cash basis for some enterprises, the accrual method for others.

4 Special accounting methods may be used by cash- or accrual-basis taxpayers to minimize the tax burden resulting from installment sales, long-term construction contracts, and revolving accounts. The entry of transactions in your journals of account is the concrete application of your accounting method to the financial facts of your business. From these journals, financial statements are created to describe the economic status of your operation, the profit pattern it enjoys, and the allocation of profit among the owners of the business.

3 • 5
A DELICATE BALANCE

Whatever accounting method you use, the principal output of your system will be three integrated reports: the balance sheet, the income statement, and the statement of owners' equity. The *balance sheet,* which is sometimes called the *statement of financial condition* or the *position statement,* recites the familiar equation,

$$\text{Assets} - \text{liabilities} = \text{owners' equity}$$

This clear interrelationship of accounting components graphically demonstrates that your creditors have claims against the assets of your business, and that your rights as an owner are only residual. Exhibit D is a simplified, but real-life, balance sheet. Let's examine it very closely and see what it really means.

What-A-Company
Statement of Financial Condition
as of January 31, 1978

(a) *Current assets:*	
(b) Cash and marketable securities	$ 1,880
(c) Accounts receivable	
(Less allowance for doubtful accounts: $300)	21,745
(d) Inventories	31,510
Prepaid expenses	915
Total current assets	56,050
(g) *Less current liabilities:*	
(h) Notes payable and current portion of long-term debt	6,223
Accounts payable and accrued expenses	11,818
U.S. and foreign income taxes	2,657
Total current liabilities	20,698
(i) *Working capital*	35,352
(e) *Other assets:*	
(f) Property, plant and equipment	28,224
Deferred charges	2,079
Excess of investment in subsidiaries over book value of net assets	5,762
Total other assets	36,065
Assets less current liabilities	71,417
(j) *Less other liabilities:*	
(k) Long-term debt	19,923
(l) Deferred taxes on income and other credits	940
Other liabilities	2,600
Total other liabilities	23,463
Excess of assets over liabilities	$47,954
(m) *Shareholders' ownership:*	
Minority interest in subsidiaries	$ 2,306
What-A-Company shareholders:	
(n) Common stock (authorized 5,000 shares of $1 par value each; issued, 2,415)	2,415
(o) Excess of shareholders' investment over par value of common stock	6,446
(p) Retained earnings	37,440
	46,301
Less treasury stock at cost (38 shares)	653
Total ownership—company shareholders	45,648
Total	$47,954

3 • 6
SUMMING UP YOUR ASSETS

Assets are everything the business owns—real estate, personalty, even intangibles. Balance sheets always divide assets into categories. See how they look in Exhibit D.

Current assets (a) are *liquid assets,* such as cash on hand (b) accounts receivable (c), and inventories (d).

Other assets (e) include *intangible assets* the business has acquired—such as organizational expense, patents, copyrights, and goodwill—and *fixed assets* or *capital assets* (f)— that is, buildings, land, machinery, and any other tangible business property with a useful life in excess of one year (except stock in trade).

3 • 7
HOW DEPRECIATION WORKS FOR YOU

For tax purposes, the cost of most intangibles may be deducted or amortized over a period of years. Similarly, capital assets (but not inventories, land, or stock in trade) are generally subject to *depreciation,* an allocation of their cost over the anticipated term of useful life. A reserve for accumulated depreciation is deducted from the costs of assets to arrive at the asset value declared on the balance sheet.

To standardize taxpayers' estimates of useful lives, the IRS has established the Class Life Asset Depreciation Range System (ADR), based on broad industry classes of assets. A taxpayer may annually elect to accept promulgated class life ranges, and thus avoid justifying his asset retirement and replacement policies.

There are three widely adopted depreciation methods:

1 *The straight-line method* recovers the cost of an asset, less any predicted salvage value, in equal annual installments over its useful life. This method lets you defer a major portion of your deduction to future years, when you may really need it.

2 Each year, the *declining-balance method* applies a uniform percentage rate (as much as twice the rate you'd use in a straight-line computation) to the asset's cost, less any de-

preciation you have already taken, until only a reasonable salvage value is left. In effect, you are given a whopping deduction in the early years of an asset's life, a deduction which is more than welcome if your income needs the offset then.

Only assets with useful lives of three years or more are eligible for declining-balance depreciation. So-called double declining balance—using twice the straight-line rate—is available only for new personal property. You are limited to 150 percent of the straight-line rate for new real estate or used personal property which is new to you. Used residential property is restricted to 125 percent of the straight-line rate.

3 *The sum-of-the-years'-digits method,* available for most personal property, is the toughest formula to apply, but may well be worth the extra effort. Add the digits in the number of years in your asset's useful life. For instance, this sum would be 10 for a machine with a four-year useful life $(1 + 2 + 3 + 4 = 10)$. Each year, you would deduct that part of your cost after salvage value represented by the fraction,

$$\frac{\text{Years of remaining useful life}}{\text{Sum of the years' digits}}$$

In this example, you would deduct 4/10 in the first year, 3/10 in the second year, 2/10 in the third year, and 1/10 in the last year of useful life. The sum-of-the-years'-digits method offers the advantage of accelerated depreciation—major deductions early on—as well as the major disadvantage inherent in any accelerated depreciation formula—*recapture* of the "excess" depreciation as ordinary taxable income upon an asset's premature disposition.

Any taxpayer except a trust may elect to write off 20 percent of the cost of tangible personal property (without reduction for salvage value) in its first year of depreciable life, in addition to regular depreciation on the balance. This *"bonus" depreciation* is limited to $10,000 of cost per year, and applies only to property with a remaining useful life of six years or more.

3•8
ALL THAT'S DUE

Liabilities are everything the business owes. Like assets, they are categorized on the balance sheet (Exhibit D):

Current liabilities (g) are debts due within one year, including short-term notes payable (h), salaries and wages payable, and dividends payable.

Contingent liabilities, those claims that may ripen through litigation, settlement, or the happening of events into full-fledged debts, would also become current liabilities, and might be footnoted here. Subtract current liabilities from current assets and you will know your total *working capital* (i).

Other liabilities (j) are *fixed liabilities* or *deferred liabilities.* These are long-term private debts (k), including bonds, notes, and mortgages payable, and deferred tax liabilities (l).

3•9
IT'S ALL YOURS

Shareholders' ownership (m) or *owners' equity* or *net worth* represents the owners' interest in a business, but not necessarily the distribution of interests upon liquidation. In a proprietorship or partnership, the equity account is merely a composite of capital contributions; retained earnings are viewed as further capital contributions, and withdrawals diminish the capital account. Corporations divide equity into stock ownership—both common (n) and preferred—and surpluses, which may be carved into credit-balance reserve accounts for the future payment of dividends to shareholders and for other prospective liabilities.

3•10
HOW ARE YOU DOING?

The *income statement* or *statement of profit and loss* (P&L) looks at the dynamic flow of your business. A whole year's activity may be summarized in terms of profit or loss. Exhibit E offers a bare-bones, but actual, income statement. Note these elements in particular:

⇒ *Net sales* (a) is your gross income, less any returns and allowances. In a service business, the label might be *operating income*.

⇒ *Cost of goods sold* (b) is a deduction from net sales, calculated by adding the *inventory*—articles held for sale to customers in the regular course of business (including production costs, if you are a manufacturer)—at the beginning of the accounting period to all purchases made during the period, and then subtracting the inventory at the close of the period. The lower the ending inventory, the lower the net profit, and the lower your income tax. That's why your identification and valuation of inventories is so closely scrutinized by the IRS.

Exhibit E

What-A-Company

Income Statement
Year Ended January 31, 1978

(a)	Net sales and operating revenues	$126,021
	Operating costs:	
(b)	Cost of goods sold	84,236
(c)	Selling and administrative expenses	28,149
	Total operating costs	112,385
(d)	Income from operations	13,636
	Sundry charges—net	2,576
	Income before taxes on income	11,060
	Taxes on income	2,765
(e)	*Net income for the year*	$ 8,295
	Average shares outstanding	2,376
(f)	*Earnings per share*	$ 3.49

The first step in computing inventories is counting or guesstimating the actual number of articles available for sale and identifying the articles still on hand—rarely an easy task. Be sure to include all finished goods, work in progress, and raw materials and supplies which have been acquired for sale or which will become part of goods to be sold. Consider any goods to which you have title, even if they are in transit. One of these inventory-identification techniques should help:

Direct matching. Each item is individually matched with its true cost or market value. Use direct matching if the sheer size of your inventory won't make it impractical.

Last in, first out (LIFO). The items most recently purchased are assumed to be the first items sold. LIFO makes sense in times of inflationary prices because the most recent and highest prices apply for valuation purposes, and the smallest profit and tax would result. Those who use LIFO must do so for both financial and tax accounting purposes, and they must value inventories at cost. A switch to LIFO requires IRS approval and fancy accounting reconciliations.

Dollar-value LIFO. This takeoff on LIFO may be used for large, homogeneous inventories. Rather than counting units, dollar-value LIFO takes the dollar value of the opening and closing inventories and adjusts to reflect the rise or fall in prices.

Retail LIFO. Popular with large retail outlets, retail LIFO is similar to dollar-value LIFO in theory, but is based on retail prices adjusted for markups and markdowns.

First in, first out (FIFO). The reverse of LIFO, this method assumes that the first items purchased are the first items sold. FIFO holds profits down in times of falling prices.

Once you have determined the identity and quantity of inventory items, how do you judge their worth? In general, inventories are valued in one of three ways:

1   *Cost.* This is the most common method of valuing inventories. For retail businesses, cost means what you paid plus shipping and handling charges minus discounts. For producers, cost means the total of all raw materials, overhead, labor, and other related expenses.

2   *Cost or market, whichever is lower.* The market value of pur-
    chased goods is the current prevailing price; manufac-
    turers are held to the current cost of reproducing goods.
    This method requires that each item be valued at the
    lower of cost or market value.

3   *Market.* This method is available only to dealers in securi-
    ties and some commodities.

⇒   *Selling and administrative expenses* (c) are general operating
    expenses apart from the cost of goods sold. These include
    salaries, rent, utilities, advertising costs, depreciation, and
    all kinds of other deductions which are not directly inven-
    tory related.

⇒   *Income from operations* (d) is a pretax profit figure, which
    may be supplemented by *extraordinary* or *nonoperating in-
    come* and reduced by *extraordinary* or *nonoperating expenses.*

⇒   *Net income for the year* (e) is the bottom-line report of your
    success, which may then be allocated among the owners of
    your business (f). Net income is carried forward to the
    balance sheet as a credit to the owners' equity account and
    as a corresponding debit to fixed or current assets, or a
    combination of both, depending upon the destination of
    your profit dollars.

3•11
YOUR PIECE OF THE PIE

The *statement of owners' equity* or *statement of retained earnings* is
the third basic piece in your accounting system. Although
form and complexity vary dramatically, this report will always
show the owners' rights at the beginning and at t⁻e end of the
subject period, and it will account for the difference. Note
these principal calculations in Exhibit F:

⇒   *Retained earnings, starting balance* (a). A proprietorship or
    partnership would show the balance in the owners' equity
    account on the first day of the period. However captioned,
    this is the starting point.

⇒   *Net profits and contributions* (b). Add any net operating
    profit, earnings from investments, and owners' capital
    contributions.

Exhibit F

```
┌─────────────────────────────────────────────────────────────┐
│                    What-A-Company                            │
│                                                              │
│               Statement of Retained Earnings                 │
│               Year Ended January 31, 1978                    │
│                                                              │
│                                                              │
│  (a) Retained earnings, beginning as previously              │
│        reported                              $29,145         │
│  (b) Net income for the year                   8,295         │
│  (c) Dividends                                   —           │
│                                              ─────────        │
│  (d) Retained earnings, ending               $37,440         │
│                                              ═════════        │
└─────────────────────────────────────────────────────────────┘
```

⇒ *Losses and withdrawals* (c). Deduct any net operating loss, casualty loss, distributions to owners as withdrawals or dividends, and retained earnings capitalized as stock.

⇒ *Retained earnings, ending balance* (d). This is the dollars-and-cents response to the inescapable question, "What have I got?"

3•12
WHAT DOES IT ALL MEAN?

Successful business managers universally agree that the better informed their decision making is, the more effective it is apt to be. Your intelligent and thoughtful interpretation of financial data should pay off handsomely:

⇒ Comparisons will guide you. See how you fared this year as compared with last year; you'll see your growth in its logical context. See how one profit center scored against another; expose your weaknesses and correct or eliminate them. See how you did in comparison with the competition; learn from their mistakes and their victories.

⇒ Rely on *ratio analysis*. Comparing one accounting element with another can reveal nearly everything about the real condition of a business. Check these key ratios in your enterprise:

— *Working capital.* The ratio of current assets to liabilities will tell you how easily you meet your immediate obligations. To be conservative, subtract inventories from current assets in assessing your bill-paying ability.

— *Net income to net worth.* This is the percentage of return on invested capital, especially important to you as an investor.

— *Net profit to net sales.* This is a test of profitability. If you fall short of the competition, insist on a *cost accounting* analysis to learn why.

⇒ Treat financial statements as educational building blocks. Graduate to specialized reports which will offer a closer look at acute problems. And focus on data particularly interesting or important to shareholders or potential investors. Consider monthly sales analyses, analyses of production costs, and any other reports that will prove useful to you as you direct the growth of your business and attract support in that effort.

⇒ Use what you learn. Don't slap backs with shining financial reports; seek out danger signs. Watch for top-heavy fixed assets, uncontrolled liabilities, excessive inventories—and act. Possibly no one else will.

4

DEVELOPING SOMETHING SPECIAL

The man with a new idea is a crank until the idea succeeds.

—Samuel Langhorne Clemens

4 • 1
A FEW DEFINITIONS

Good ideas are a vital force in the growth of any successful business. Understandably, you will want to preserve the unique business ideas you create. Yet pure thought cannot be owned by anyone—not by you and not by your competition. The law will protect a property right in ideas only when those ideas have been reduced to a recognizable form or expression. Here are the most common ways to establish such intellectual property:

⇒ A *patent* is the exclusive right to use, manufacture, and sell the concrete expression of a novel and useful idea or design. Governed by federal law, patents are granted for limited time periods prescribed by statute.

⇒ Business know-how and, in fact, any confidential information you maintain for the good of your business may qualify as a *trade secret*. Trade secrets are protected by common-law concepts embodied in state laws. These laws

50

prohibit others from wrongfully breaching such secrecy, either through the commission of a tort or the violation of an express or implied contract.

⇒ A common-law, or statutory, *copyright* protects literary and artistic property from unauthorized reproduction or performance.

⇒ A word, name, symbol, or device used to distinguish and identify your product by indicating its origin may be registered under state and federal laws as a *trademark*. A trademark serves to guarantee a product's quality and indeed creates and sustains a demand for the product.

⇒ In the end, a commercial *contract* between the creator and the user of intellectual property will invariably fix and assure its value.

4•2
PATENT PREREQUISITES

Although a patent will exclude others from using, manufacturing, and selling your product without your authority, it will not safeguard your invention's secrecy, nor will it prevent other inventors from improving on your idea and patenting their own "new" products. Even your rights to exclusivity will expire in 3½ to 17 years, leaving your product idea vulnerable to expropriation. Nonetheless, a patent is probably the best protection available to an inventor. See if you meet the following three requirements:

1 *You must be the original inventor.* Obviously, you may not receive a patent on someone else's brainstorm. And even if the idea is your own, it may lose its patentability after others gain access to it, perhaps through descriptions in print or through public use.

2 *Your idea must be novel, nonobvious, and concrete in form.* Only a utilitarian application of an idea can be patented, not the naked idea itself. So scientific principles like Einstein's theory of relativity just don't qualify. Neither do concepts or combinations of concepts that are old hat, nor solutions that might occur to just anyone. Yet an idea need not be mysterious to be judged nonobvious: a safety pin, for in-

stance, seems like a very obvious answer to an age-old
need, but only after you've seen one.

3 *Your idea must fall into one of the three patentable categories:
Utility inventions* (any new and useful process, machine,
manufacture or composition of matter), *ornamental designs*
(any design that is both useful and ornamental, such as a
new auto bumper or football helmet), or *asexually repro-
ducible plants.*

4 • 3
PATENT PROCEDURES

Having satisfied yourself that your idea appears patentable,
bring in an attorney. The Patent Office requires even lawyers
to get a special license. In fact, most patent practitioners have
both legal and engineering training. A competent specialist
will guide you through the incredibly tedious patent process:

First, you'll need to reduce your invention to written form,
in precise verbal and pictorial detail. To prove you were the
first inventor of the product you define, you'll need to establish the date of your invention. All this material will be sent to
the Patent Office as a *disclosure document,* where it will be held
confidentially for two years while you seek to secure your
patent. This procedure will help establish your invention date.

The next step is a private patent search conducted by special researchers in Washington, trained in the issues of patentability. After concluding that your invention is patentable,
your attorney will file an application on your behalf, along
with the necessary fee.

Finally, the Patent Office will issue its *office action,* accepting
or rejecting your application. Should it be rejected, you will
have three months to clarify or improve your filing. If your
application is rejected again, an administrative appeal will be
your recourse.

4 • 4
PATENT PECULIARITIES

Once you have obtained your *notice of allowance* and, ultimately, your patent, you'll enjoy all the exclusive rights it

confers. Protect those rights by respecting the laws that will now govern your invention:

⇒ Don't forget to mark your product or its package with the word "Patented" (or "Pat.") and the patent number. Patent marking constitutes legal notice to a would-be infringer, notice that will support a suit for damages. But be aware that markings such as "Patent pending" or "Patent applied for" serve only to inform the public of your intent and are frequently adopted for dubious promotional purposes. They have no legal effect because patent rights commence only with the patent's issuance and are never retroactive.

⇒ Watch out for antitrust problems. Using, licensing, or assigning a patent in any way that unlawfully restrains trade, fixes prices, or reduces competition may be grounds for the termination of your patent rights. (See section 5 • 1)

⇒ At all times, remember that your rights are controlled by the federal government, so don't treat the patent as your absolute property. Should you sell your patent, for instance, the transaction must be reported to the Patent Office within three months, or your purchaser will not succeed to your rights.

4 • 5
YOU'VE GOT A SECRET

The patent laws offer only a limited solution to your big need for intellectual property protection. Most business ideas are simply not patentable. Those that are may not be ripe for the public disclosure our patent laws require. And, sometimes most important, patents can be very costly.

Often a better answer is reliance on various state trade secret laws, which protect the owners of business secrets by guaranteeing their right to privacy and by guarding against betrayals of confidence by associates and employees. Anyone is free to use your secret, but only after discovering it fairly or developing it independently. Unlike a patented product or idea whose substance is reserved to its creator after public disclosure, a trade secret derives its very vitality from the fact that it is not disclosed. The legal protection afforded trade secrets thus hinges on your ability to show that your idea is worth protecting and that you intend to preserve its secrecy. Keep these three points in mind:

1   Protect only those secrets worth protecting. If outsiders already know what you know, or if they can gain your knowledge with little effort, protective measures are futile.
2   Limit access to genuinely valuable information—customer lists, plans, processes, formulas, any ideas that set you apart from your competition. Only those employees who need to know secrets should be able to learn them, and they should be required to respect the confidentiality of your trade secrets.
3   Demand that all personnel sign *restrictive covenants,* which might be incorporated into their employment contracts. Such covenants would acknowledge that the employer has developed and owns information that is to be treated confidentially, and that this information may be divulged to the employees who agree to keep it secret and to return any confidential documents in their possession when their employment is concluded.

4•6
COPYRIGHTING YOUR WRITING AND MORE

Copyrights offer the best protection for literary and artistic intellectual property. Unlike patents and trade secrets, a copyright relates to the exact form of expression, not the substantive idea it represents. For this reason, the copyright becomes valuable only when the form itself is worth preserving, as in the case of poetry, music, art, or advertising copy.

The Federal Copyright Act now preempts most common law copyrights for any work fixed in a tangible medium of expression. Prior registration thus becomes a condition to any infringement action for statutory damages and attorneys'

fees. The copyright owner is generally assured that his work
will not be copied, reproduced, or performed without his authority. These rights are not affirmatively granted by any government agency, but are secured by the creator who complies
with the copyright laws. Here are the requirements:

1   The material must be subject to copyright. Ideas, systems,
    and methods do not qualify; only forms of expression can
    be protected. Other ineligibles are slogans, titles, symbols,
    names, works that merely record information (such as
    diaries and address books), and works that contain only
    universally known information (including calendars and
    rulers).
2   The material must be original and must fall into one of
    these classes:

Class A	Books
Class B	Periodicals
Class C	Lectures or similar productions prepared for oral presentation
Class D	Dramatic compositions
Class E	Musical compositions
Class F	Maps
Class G	Works of art, or models or designs for works of art
Class H	Reproductions of works of art
Class I	Drawings or sculptural works of a scientific or technical nature
Class J	Photographs
Class K	Prints, pictorial illustrations, and commercial prints or labels
Class L	Motion-picture photoplays
Class M	Motion pictures other than photoplays
Class N	Sound recordings
Class O	Choreographic and pantomime works

3   The work must be fixed in a tangible medium of expres-
    sion (usually a copy or phonographic record).
4   Copies of the material must be produced with a *copyright
    notice* in the prescribed position. Generally, the notice will

consist of the word "Copyright," the abbreviation "Copr.," or the universally recognized symbol ©; the copyright owner's name; and the year of publication—

© Creative Prodigy 1978

5 Your claim should be registered in the Copyright Office. The application for registration, which varies with the class or work, must be accompanied by two copies of the best edition of the work as published (or one copy if it is to remain unpublished) and a registration fee. The process is a simple one; the specifics are available to you by writing to the Register of Copyrights, Library of Congress, Washington, D.C. 20559.

4 • 7
COPYRIGHTS AND WRONGS

The proper registration of your copyright will entitle you to protection for 50 years beyond your lifetime, during which time you and your heirs may license, mortgage, bequeath, and even sell your work. You will be recognized as the independent and original creator of the work, and others will be prohibited from using your property without your authority.

Even so, a copyright is far from perfect protection. Your rights will be limited in these ways:

⇒ The burden of proving an unauthorized use or *infringement* rests with you. You must prove that the infringer had access to your work and actually used it.

⇒ Moreover, some uses of your copyrighted work will be permitted, even in the absence of your authority. For example, the private and incidental use of your material is a permissible *fair use.* The general enjoyment and diffusion of knowledge—as opposed to its commercial exploitation—is encouraged by the courts. Recording rights in musical works are restricted by *compulsory license,* which automatically authorizes recordings of a composition (upon the payment of royalties) as soon as the composer OK's the initial recording of the work.

⇒ Finally, a copyright will neither protect the content of your work—ideas are not copyrightable—nor its exclusivity. The Copyright Office makes no search of its records to see if a similar or even identical filing has been made by someone else.

4•8
TRADING WITH TRADEMARKS

The legal protection of a *trademark* stems from the laws against "unfair competition" in business, and not from any individual ownership rights. This being the case, the registration of a trademark alone will not qualify it for protection; only its commercial use will ensure your trademark rights.

As with any commercially valuable asset, you will strive to develop trademarks that will enhance your business image. After all, the trademark's function is to identify a product and to create and maintain a demand for it. You and your attorney will seek to enhance your goodwill in the selection of trademarks, and you should avoid these pitfalls:

x Steer clear of initials and third-party names. The names or signature of any living person cannot be used without his consent.

x Avoid using any federal or state symbol and the name or likeness of a deceased U.S. president whose widow is still alive.

x Opt for a name or symbol that's suggestive, rather than descriptive. Better yet, choose one that's wholly original. Any mark that's deceptively similar to an existing mark is an invitation to a lawsuit. For this reason and others, your counsel may wisely suggest a trademark search.

x And, of course, shun any mark that is immoral or scandalous in nature.

4•9
WHY FEDERAL TRADEMARKS ARE BETTER THAN STATE

The Lanham Act permits federal registration of any trademark used in interstate commerce. Many local businesses, especially service businesses, will be limited to protection under state law, since they do not qualify under the Act. Those that do are well advised to follow through with federal registration. Here's why:

- ✔ Federal trademark laws have been liberally expanded to include *service marks* (used to identify services rather than goods), *certification marks* (third-party marks such as union-made labels used to certify origin, materials, manufacturing processes or overall quality), and *collective marks* (service or trademarks used by cooperatives or organizations to signify membership).
- ✔ Federal registration gives nationwide protection in blocking the later registration of deceptively similar marks by others.
- ✔ Federal registration prevents the importation of any goods bearing a deceptively similar mark.
- ✔ Federal registration grants the registrant the broader and often better protection the federal courts offer.

4 • 10
REGISTERING YOUR MARK

For these reasons, if your business qualifies as interstate commerce, you will certainly want to register your marks with the U.S. Commissioner of Patents. Consider making application for the *Principal Register* or the *Supplemental Register*.

The *Principal Register* is limited to "technical marks," those that are coined, arbitrary, fanciful, or suggestive. Excluded are those based on descriptive names and surnames, unless they have been in commercial use for five years or more and have clearly become identified with your product or service. Only the *Principal Register* issues notice to the world, rejecting deceptively similar marks on imports. Registration is for twenty years, renewable for additional twenty-year periods indefinitely.

The *Supplemental Register* is for marks that have been used for a year or more and are capable of distinguishing goods, but do not qualify for the *Principal Register*. The *Supplemental Register's* standards are broader, allowing any symbol, label, package, configuration of goods, word, slogan, phrase, surname, geographical name, numeral, or device. Although notice of ownership is not construed from supplemental registration, it does establish the right to sue in U.S. courts. Registration is good for twenty years and cannot be renewed, except to support a foreign registration.

Your application for registration can be filed only after your trademark is used in interstate commerce. Many times, this means preparing a label bearing the mark, affixing it to the product, and consummating a token sale across state lines. The mark is then officially in interstate use, and the application for registration can be filed. In brief, these are the filing requirements:

1   A written application must be completed. Exhibit G cites various classes of goods and services. Find yours and enter it on the application blank, which you can obtain (along with instructions) from the Commissioner of Patents, Washington, D.C. 20231.
2   Your application must be accompanied by a drawing of the mark, in India ink on white paper. Colors should be indicated by the Patent Office's color codes. If you cannot execute a finished drawing, the Patent Office will accept a crude one and will, for a fee, bring it up to legal standards.
3   With your application, you will also need to submit 5 specimens of the mark. These should be duplicates of actual labels, tags, or containers, unless specimens are impractical, in which event photos can be substituted.
4   A registration fee will be required.

Once your application is approved, either on initial examination or subsequent reexamination or after an appeal to the Trademark Trial and Appeal Board, the official *Gazette* will publish your mark. Anyone who believes your mark constitutes an infringement of an existing mark will have 30 days to protest. Protests are heard by the Trial and Appeal Board in an *interference proceeding.*

Exhibit G. Trademark classifications (by grade and title).

Goods

1. Raw or partly prepared materials
2. Receptacles
3. Baggage, animal equipments, portfolios, and pocketbooks
4. Abrasives and polishing materials
5. Adhesives
6. Chemicals and chemical compositions
7. Cordage
8. Smokers' articles, not including tobacco products
9. Explosives, firearms, equipments, and projectiles
10. Fertilizers
11. Inks and inking materials
12. Construction materials
13. Hardware and plumbing and steamfitting supplies
14. Metals and metal castings and forgings
15. Oils and greases
16. Protective and decorative coatings
17. Tobacco products
18. Medicines and pharmaceutical preparations
19. Vehicles
20. Linoleum and oiled cloth
21. Electrical apparatus, machines, and supplies
22. Games, toys, and sporting goods
23. Cutlery, machinery, and tools, and parts thereof
24. Laundry appliances and machines
25. Locks and safes
26. Measuring and scientific appliances
27. Horological instruments
28. Jewelry and precious metal ware
29. Brooms, brushes, and dusters
30. Crockery, earthenware, and porcelain
31. Filters and refrigerators
32. Furniture and upholstery
33. Glassware
34. Heating, lighting, and ventilating apparatus
35. Belting, hose, machinery packing, and nonmetallic tires
36. Musical instruments and supplies
37. Paper and stationery
38. Prints and publications
39. Clothing
40. Fancy goods, furnishings, and notions
41. Canes, parasols, and umbrellas
42. Knitted, netted, and textile fabrics, and substitutes therefor
43. Thread and yarn
44. Dental, medical, and surgical appliances
45. Soft drinks and carbonated waters
46. Foods and ingredients of foods
47. Wines
48. Malt beverages and liquors
49. Distilled alcoholic liquors
50. Merchandise not otherwise classified
51. Cosmetics and toilet preparations
52. Detergents and soaps

Services

100. Miscellaneous
101. Advertising and business
102. Insurance and financial
103. Construction and repair
104. Communication
105. Transportation and storage
106. Material treatment
107. Education and entertainment

Collective Membership

200. Collective membership

4 • 11

YOUR CONTINUING TRADEMARK OBLIGATIONS

If no protests are lodged, or if all protests are resolved in your favor, you will ultimately receive a *certificate of registration,* entitling your goods to carry the legend "Registered in U.S. Patent Office," or "Reg. U.S. Pat. Off.," or the familiar symbol, ®. It will then become your ongoing obligation to preserve that privilege in all the following ways:

⇒ *Use your trademark properly.* Display the mark (exactly as registered) distinctly and conspicuously to identify your goods. Use it consistently to modify the generic name, with no words between them. If it's a word, always capitalize it and use it as an adjective, never as a noun or verb. "Thermos" and "cellophane" were lost as trademarks because their owners failed to distinguish them as brands rather than generic terms. And by all means, use the mark continually: disuse can be labeled an abandonment of the mark and of your rights to it.

⇒ *Protect your mark.* Be on the lookout for any potential and actual infringements and report them. Check the official *Gazette* each week, or have your lawyer do it, and file a timely protest against any similar mark in a pending application.

⇒ *File the affidavits you need.* An *Affidavit* or *Declaration of Use* must be filed with the Patent Office during the sixth year after registration. This document must include the number and date of your certificate of registration and an affirmation that the mark—a sample of which should be attached—is still in use. Failure to comply will result in cancellation of your registration.

Under certain circumstances, you can also file an *Affidavit* or *Declaration of Incontestability.* This filing would firmly establish your rights in your mark and exempt it from interference proceedings before the Trial and Appeal Board. An affidavit may be submitted only after the mark has been registered and continuously used for five years, and only if the registrant has received no adverse decision concerning its right to use the mark and there is no pending proceeding on that point.

⇒ *Renew your rights.* Marks on the *Principal Register* must be renewed during the last half of the twentieth year. The renewal application includes roughly the same information as the Affidavit of Use and should be accompanied by the statutory fee.

⇒ *Register any change in ownership.* If the mark is sold, even as part of the business goodwill, this change calls for registration. The new owner will succeed to the unexpired portion of the original term of registration.

4 • 12
CONTRACTING WITH THE CREATIVE

In addition to the intellectual property you develop, you will no doubt want to use and protect the applied ideas of employees, independent consulting contractors, and even outsiders with no relationship to the enterprise. Here are a few ways your business can best deal with the creative work done for you by other people:

1 *Intellectual property created by an employee* will be owned by him, unless his employment agreement provides otherwise. Nevertheless, you will gain a *shop right* to use any property developed at work with employer materials, and you can establish even clearer rights by having your employees contractually assign to you any inventions they may create in the course of employment.

2 *Intellectual property created by a consultant* should become yours through a carefully drafted agreement, specifically assigning to you all the ideas and inventions developed in the course of his service and binding him to keep his discoveries secret from the outside world. At the same time, he can contract not to divulge any confidential information he may learn while rendering his services.

3 *Intellectual property created by an outsider* can impose serious legal liabilities on the business that uses it without having received a written release like this one:

June 1, 1978

Through the attached descriptions and sketches, I, Genuine Genius, hereby voluntarily disclose to Yourgood Company my design for the "Brand-New Widget." This disclosure was unsolicited by Yourgood Company, which is not obligated to adopt my submission in any way. The company may retain any material I submit, and it may make copies of such material to preserve the record. No confidential relationship is created by this disclosure or by any prior or subsequent disclosure. All my rights and Yourgood Company's obligations are expressly limited to those provided by the United States Patent Statutes, yet Yourgood Company does not hereby obtain a license under any patent rights by this submission.

[signed] Genuine Genius

4 • 13
GROWING DEFENSIVELY

The legal safeguards afforded intellectual property are indispensable as the fledgling business, or even the mature one, seeks to cope with well-entrenched rivals for the sales dollar. Be vigilant, and periodically review all the ideas and applications that are important to you as well as all those likely to become important to you in the future. Then work with your lawyer in fortifying your creative line of defense against your most vigorous competitors.

5

SELLING YOUR WARES

We demand that . . . business give the people a square deal; in return, we must insist that when anyone engaged in . . . business honestly endeavors to do right, he shall himself be given a square deal.

—Theodore Roosevelt

5•1
THE ANTITRUST PHILOSOPHY

Our economic system is one of free enterprise, and businesses are encouraged to compete freely and to contract independently. Nonetheless, your relationships with both competitors and customers are governed by a battery of federal and state antitrust laws, enacted to regulate the marketing and distribution of goods and services. For the most part, federal antitrust laws are enforced by the Federal Trade Commission and the Department of Justice. Although the laws themselves are very complex, their basic purposes are easily understood.

⇒ The *Sherman Antitrust Act* seeks to ensure the survival of a competitive, capitalist economy. The Act bars unreasonable restraints that would threaten open competition and thereby tend to create monopolies. Businesses are specifically prohibited from engaging in activities that would unduly restrain others from competing freely—

boycotts, price-fixing, tying agreements (section 1•13), and now even fair trading.

⇒ The *Clayton Act,* amended by the *Robinson-Patman Act* and the *Cellar-Kefauver Act,* guarantees the right of the small business to compete. The Act prohibits discrimination by reason of size or economic power, and outlaws tactics such as unjust price discrimination, total requirements contracts, and the monopolistic acquisition of competitors.

⇒ The *Federal Trade Commission Act* defends the public's right to choose among competing goods and services on the basis of their true merit.

Thus the antitrust laws regulate you, but they regulate your competitors too. The result is a competitive climate in which the small business can exist and thrive. Your growth must be deliberate, but always sensitive to the rights of both your competitors and the public. So—

You may . . .	But you may not . . .
Freely choose your customers and suppliers.	Refuse to deal unless they meet illegal tying, price-fixing, or territory-carving demands.
Enter into reasonable resale or distributorship agreements.	Go beyond what is reasonable to ensure that you can survive and compete. So avoid unduly restrictive agreements, especially with businesses smaller than yours.
Sell the same product under different brands at different prices, offer different qualities of goods at different prices, and sell the same goods at different prices to different classes of customers.	Use pricing to discriminate or compete unfairly (1) by offering the same goods to the same class of customers at different prices (or with other benefits offered to one and not the other) or (2) by coercing suppliers into giving you preferential price treatment or other inducements.

Use any fair means to out do your competition.	Use predatory tactics, such as bribing your competitors' employees or disparaging their goods and services, excluding them from a market through restrictive contracts, or initiating price wars in order to drive them out of business.
Be friendly with the competition and join them in trade associations and industrywide service organizations.	Cooperate with the competition to limit prices or product, to divide markets, or to initiate boycotts or blacklists.

The antitrust aspects of marketing are so detailed and pervasive that we can only hope to convey their flavor here. Antimonopoly provisions of the antitrust laws are explored more fully in section 11•8.

5•2
SOME ADVERTISING IDEAS

Just as the methods of marketing your goods and services will be regulated from beginning to end, the way your wares are portrayed to the public will also be closely scrutinized by officials at every level of government. Although countless federal acts specifically affect advertising—among them the Communications Act, the Federal Food, Drug and Cosmetics Act, the Consumer Credit Protection Act, the Consumer Products Safety Act, the Trademarks Act, and the Copyright Act—it is the Federal Trade Commission Act that probably has the most powerful impact on business in general. The Federal Trade Commission's powers to prevent unfair competition and deceptive practices in or affecting interstate commerce give it considerable control over advertising content. The Commission's mandate is to monitor radio and television broadcasts of commercial messages, to review ads in print media, and to hear consumer and business complaints, all with a view toward eradicating injury through advertising.

The consumer's right to truth and accountability has caused the FTC to promulgate rules and regulations covering not only how a product is advertised and sold, but also how it performs after the consumer takes it home. The following are a few basic principles that govern the interpretation of "unfair and deceptive practices" and that should be considered in the formulation of your advertising program:

1 *An advertisement must not tend to mislead or deceive* either by picture or word. Whether your ad actually does mislead or deceive is not the issue. Exaggeration is now held to very strict limits and is acceptable only when it is clearly a statement of opinion—such as "the most beautiful" or "the best tasting"—and not a representation of fact.

2 *Foreknowledge or intent to deceive* on the part of the advertiser *is not necessary* to prove that an advertisement violates FTC standards.

3 *The contents of an ad will be judged in light of the impression it makes on the public.* Recent decisions look at advertisements as the average consumer, one who is credulous and gullible, might. Worse still, advertising to a particular market—the very young or the uneducated, for instance—is examined in light of that specific audience's lesser capacity to understand it.

4 *The advertiser is held to his express and implied warranties.* So, to the extent that you can, you will want to limit your commitments.

5•3
YOUR HIDDEN WARRANTIES

As goods pass from the manufacturer to the distributor to the dealer and ultimately to the consumer, all kinds of warranties might be expressed. And the courts, finding *implied* or *apparent authority* for statements made, have held parties who are early in the distributive chain liable for the overzealous claims of sales personnel. Even in the absence of an express warranty, the Uniform Commercial Code recognizes two kinds of implied warranties:

1 *The implied warranty of merchantability* means that goods should be fit for the ordinary purposes for which they are used: food should be edible; automobiles should run.

2 *The implied warranty of fitness for a particular purpose* means that a buyer has a right to rely on a seller's skill or judgment in selecting or furnishing goods that will satisfy the buyer's special needs. For example, if a seller knows that a customer needs shoes for mountain climbing, his sale of a certain pair for that purpose creates a warranty of fitness.

Many jurisdictions hold sellers and manufacturers liable for injuries resulting from design or manufacturing defects where neither negligence nor breach of warranty can be found. Such product liability cases are now running a million a year! And sound marketing practices and disclaimers of warranty can do little to avoid "strict liability." What's more, the law labels the contractual limitation of damages for personal injuries from consumer goods as "unconscionable" and generally unenforceable.

Your liability for a product's repair or replacement and for damages of a commercial nature may be limited by a conspicuous and timely disclaimer. The FTC is empowered by the Magnuson-Moss Act to issue regulations dealing both with disclaimers in written warranties and with minimum standards for warranty provisions. And the Commission is dedicated to exacting full disclosure of the terms of any warranty.

Written warranties on products selling for more than $10 must be clearly designated as "limited" or "full." A full warranty remedies any defect, malfunction, or failure without charge to the customer, honors any implied warranty, and allows the purchaser a replacement or refund if repairs prove unsuccessful. Warranties must disclose who can enforce them, which parts of a product are actually warranted, which characteristics of each part are covered and which are not, their terms, any limitation on the implied warranties of merchantability and fitness for a particular use (in limited warranties), and any limitation on responsibility for consequential or incidental damages (in limited warranties). A statement of warranty rights must also be included:

THIS WARRANTY GIVES YOU SPECIFIC LEGAL RIGHTS AND YOU
MAY ALSO HAVE OTHER RIGHTS WHICH MAY VARY FROM STATE
TO STATE.

5•4
A FEW FTC SPECIFICS

As we have seen, the philosophy of the FTC is to protect the
consumer. The theory deserves some practical amplification.
Note these specific practices which the FTC has recently
criticized:

x   Don't imply that your widget is a product of Big Corpo-
    ration unless it is.
x   Don't confuse your audience with misleading endorse-
    ments. Claiming that "Doctors recommend Vitamin–
    Tab" can only get you in trouble if the "doctor" you are
    quoting happens to be your brother-in-law.
x   Don't foster misunderstandings about your association
    with another concern. Pretending that your repair shop
    is an official Major Company outlet is wishful thinking
    that can backfire.
x   Don't exaggerate your product's benefits. You will prob-
    ably be able to sell your mouthwash just as well, even if it
    cannot cure the common cold.
x   Don't misrepresent your product's origin. Your "imports"
    had better be genuine.
x   Don't label goods "new" when they aren't. A product is
    generally "new" for only six months.
x   Don't contend that your product meets a standard unless
    you can prove it. Avoid unequivocal words like "best,"
    "colorfast," and "aged"; the consumer may have a right
    to take you literally.
x   Don't misstate the quantity of goods available. Your "lim-
    ited supply" must be just that, or you are exercising
    undue pressure on the consumer.
x   Don't disparage a competitor. "Commercial freedom of
    speech" encourages comparative advertising, but it de-
    mands a complete and accurate presentation.

x Don't advertise a loss leader without intending to meet a reasonable public demand unless you also communicate the fact that quantities are limited.

x Don't advertise a "Going-Out-of-Business Sale" unless you are closing your doors. And hold no "Fire Sale" unless you have suffered a fire.

5•5
WHERE CREDIT IS DUE

The principles of full disclosure become even more concrete in the area of credit (Chapter 6). The federal Truth-in-Lending Act demands standardized formats and language in the advertisement of all consumer credit (except in connection with residential real estate, where similar but different rules apply). Once you offer "24 months to pay" or "$20 down," you subject your advertisement to the Act's requirements, including these restrictions:

x To protect the consumer from "bait" advertising, an advertiser is prohibited from offering to extend credit to buyers unless he customarily arranges such terms.

x An advertiser may not offer "no down payment" or any specific down payment unless he will accept those terms.

x Any advertisement which seeks to promote credit, but where the seller is not imposing a specific finance charge, must clearly state that "The cost of credit is included in the price quoted for the goods and services."

x Any ad offering "open-end credit" (including revolving charge accounts and credit cards) must comply with your state's usury law and "clearly and conspicuously" disclose:

1 The annual percentage rates of finance charge and the range of unpaid balances to which these rates will be applied.

2 The time period, if any, within which the balance may be paid off without a finance charge.

3 The method used to compute finance charges and the range of balances to which they are applied.

x   Any ad offering loans or installment sales must comply
with your state's usury law and must "clearly and conspicuously" disclose:
1   The cash price or the amount of the loan.
2   The amount of the finance charge, given as an annual percentage rate.
3   The amount of the down payment, or that no down
payment is required.
4   The number, amount, and date of repayments.
5   The deferred payment price or the sum of the payments, whichever applies.

5•6
REGULATIONS GALORE

The FTC's promulgations are complex and voluminous.
They are all available from the Bureau of Information, Federal Trade Commission, Washington, D.C. 20580. Be sure to
stay on the safe side of these proscriptions too:

x   Many state laws—notably the *Uniform Deceptive Trade
Practice and Consumer Protection Act*—pick up where FTC
guidelines leave off. False and misleading advertising
thus becomes the rightful prey of two levels of
government.
x   The states also regulate the advertisement of securities,
banks, professions, insurance—you name it.
x   Federal postal laws prohibit using the mails to perpetuate
a fraud, to transmit obscene or lascivious matter, to incite
certain crimes, and to promote lotteries. Remember that
almost all newspapers and magazines are distributed
through the mail, thus subjecting their contents to postal
inquiry.
x   The federal government has all kinds of special powers
to regulate particular industries, and that power is
broadly exercised. The Internal Revenue Service, for instance, regulates the advertising of alcoholic beverages;
the Federal Communications Commission regulates
radio and TV broadcasts; the Securities and Exchange

Commission regulates the advertising of stocks and bonds.

x   Ads are subject to slander and libel laws. Be sure of your facts and your legal authority to use them.

x   The Robinson-Patman Act prohibits a seller from paying a buyer for a service the buyer furnishes unless that payment is also made available to the buyer's competitors. A seller may not discriminate in favor of one buyer over another. So cooperative advertising programs ought to be made known equally to all competing customers.

x   Lotteries—involving prizes, consideration, and chance—constitute unfair competition under both federal and state laws. That is why advertisers using such promotional devices seek to avoid either consideration ("no purchase need be made") or chance ("duplicate prizes will be awarded in the event of a tie").

5 • 7
HANDLING THE FREELANCER

Once you decide what your ad may say and what it may not, the remaining legal objective is your protection in disseminating that information. First, you will want to clarify your relationship with any artist, copywriter, or photographer you hire. Before ink is put to paper, have your lawyer draft a simple letter agreement covering these points:

⇒   Your contractor must warrant that everything he submits to you is his own work.

⇒   You gain legal rights over any material your contractor develops on your time. Have him specifically assign his rights in any creative work he speculatively developed for you before you hired him.

⇒   Have your contractor acknowledge your exclusive right to copyright his work. (See sections 4 • 6 and 4 • 7)

⇒   Set yourself up as the sole arbiter of what is acceptable work and what is not.

⇒ Require that releases be obtained before pictures or testimonials are used. Invasion of privacy can give rise to a lawsuit.

5•8
YOUR CONTRACT WITH THE MEDIA

After an ad is developed, the publishing or broadcasting of it will create additional rights and obligations. As an advertiser, you will be called upon to present your title to all material you submit. You will agree to submit copy and artwork and to pay for your ad on time. Finally, you will be expected to avoid statements that violate FTC and similar standards.

Here is what the media will do for you:

1   They are obliged to provide time and space in a fair and impartial manner.
2   They must charge equal and fair rates to all advertisers. A couple of exceptions: frequency discounts and long-run discounts are permitted, as are surcharges for short-term runs.
3   They are duty-bound to perform accurately. The media can be held liable for your out-of-pocket loss and any loss in goodwill that results from their errors. But liability is uniformly limited by contract to a small dollar amount, and you are obligated to mitigate whatever damage you suffer.

5•9
HIRING AN AGENCY

Many companies assume still another contractual relationship in advertising their products—the retention of an advertising agency. Unfortunately, the creative professionalism one can buy in an agency accomplishes little in the way of exculpation for the advertising sins this chapter has explored. As the principal, your company will retain ultimate control over your agent and, with it, ultimate liability for whatever your agent does and says on your behalf. Most agencies are painstaking in preserving their good names by assuring fairness and honesty in all they present to the public, but you will remain responsible for your ad's contents. This being the case, what legal protections of competency are you actually guaranteed?

- ✔ *Expertise.* You have a legal right to your agency's best efforts and greatest skill.
- ✔ *Loyalty.* Your interests come first. This means that your trade secrets (section 4•5) are not to be divulged, and that any useful information your agency learns is to be brought to your attention. It makes sense, then, that your agency may not represent the competition unless both you and your competitor agree.
- ✔ *Obedience.* You have a right to your agent's full cooperation. All your instructions should be carried out, unless they are illegal or clearly unreasonable.
- ✔ *Fiduciary responsibility.* Your agent may not "self-deal," nor may it unilaterally contract out your work to another of its clients. What is more, any expense money you deposit with your agent must be segregated and used to pay only the bills you authorize, not the agent's general debts.
- ✔ *Fiscal honesty.* Your agent is obliged to render frequent and strict accountings to you.

5•10
THE AGENCY CONTRACT

These principles take on practical significance in the formal contract between agent and client. Its major provisions should include these:

- ⇒ *A description of the services the agency is to perform and its fee for those services.* Note the way fees are computed: Are they straight commissions? or media cost plus an incremental percentage of media costs for profit? or media cost plus an hourly rate? or what?
- ⇒ *Disbursement guidelines.* What authority is required prior to an expense payout? To whom are disbursements to be made?

⇒ *Status reports and approval.* Do you retain the right to approve each component within a campaign?

⇒ *Deadlines.* Are they realistic and do they conform to the seasonal nature of your business?

⇒ *Billing procedures.* Do payment dates reasonably correspond to completion dates? What credit terms, if any, are you given?

⇒ *Discounts.* Does the agency agree to take advantage of all discounts and pass the savings on to the advertiser?

⇒ *The ownership of ideas.* Is the advertiser acknowledged as the sole owner of all material developed, even that which isn't used?

⇒ *Fiduciary duties.* Are they all spelled out?

⇒ *Indemnification.* Where the advertiser and agency may be jointly liable, would you be compelled to hold the agency harmless?

⇒ *Term.* What is the duration of the contract? How much notice must be given to terminate it?

5•11
A PERSONAL CODE

Only the most naive will assert that the statutory law of the marketplace and its morality are one. Yet, to grow successfully, you will not need legal clearance for every advertising and marketing idea that comes your way. Simply apply your own standards of fairness and honesty, and, except for the most technical points, your legal judgment will match your lawyer's.

6

GIVING THEM CREDIT

*So far as my coin would stretch; and where it would not,
I have used my credit.*

—William Shakespeare in
King Henry IV

6•1
EXPANDING YOUR PROFIT BASE

The extension of retail credit is frequently an indispensable adjunct to the sales effort. If your goods and services could be bought only by cash-on-the-barrelhead, many of your customers simply could not afford to deal with you. Others would be forced to divert their spending power into other channels with higher priorities. Rather than turn that business away, you might prefer to establish an organized credit-and-collection program. Reap the benefit of volume that you would otherwise lose, and gain additional profit from permissible finance charges on ever-growing receivables.

6•2
LIMITING YOUR EXPOSURE

The first step in the consumer-credit process is screening the credit applicant. Your selectivity in accepting credit risks is crucial to the eventual collection of monies owed you. The Equal Credit Opportunity Act sees to it that your selectivity is rational by setting these rules:

⇒ You may not discount the income your applicant draws from part-time employment.

⇒ You may not seek information about an applicant's spouse unless the spouse is to share the benefits and responsibilities of the account; and now, you must maintain separate credit histories for both a husband and wife who share an account.

⇒ You may not deny credit on the basis of sex or marital status.

⇒ Automatic rejections on account of age, religion or race will soon become the subject of similar remedial legislation.

The mass preselection of credit risks has rightfully been replaced by individual investigations into the creditworthiness of applicants. The Fair Credit Reporting Act, designed principally to regulate consumer reporting agencies, applies equally to those who request the investigative reports. Before using an investigative report, you are obliged to let your applicant know:

1   That an investigative report may be used.
2   Just what an investigative report is.
3   That he has a right to request a "complete and accurate" statement describing the type and scope of the investigation conducted. (If he exercises this right, you have five days to comply with his request.)

Exhibit H is a Federal Trade Commission disclosure form that serves the purpose.

If a credit report discloses information that causes you to deny a credit request or to increase the charge for credit, you must so advise your customer and supply him with the name and address of the agency responsible for the report. He can then challenge the completeness or accuracy of the information you have received. If a source other than a credit bureau has forwarded information that influences you to decide against the applicant, he has similar rights. Let him know that credit is denied and that he may request in writing the nature

Exhibit H. Disclosure of investigative consumer report.

[*When a separate notice is used*]
This is to inform you that as part of our procedure for processing
your credit application . . .

                              or

[*When disclosed in the application*]
In making this application for credit it is understood that . . .

an investigation may be made whereby information is obtained
through personal interviews with your neighbors, friends, or
others with whom you are acquainted. This inquiry includes information as to your character, general reputation, personal
characteristics and mode of living. You have the right to make a
written request within a reasonable period of time to receive
additional, detailed information about the nature and scope of
this investigation.

---

of the information that led to your decision. The Federal
Trade Commission suggests the format shown in Exhibit I.

6•3
THE PERVASIVE REGULATION Z

Your customers who are ultimately granted consumer credit
will probably be protected by the Federal Reserve System's
exhaustive Regulation Z, or by your state's even broader Uniform Consumer Credit Code. Where enacted, the UCCC
takes the place of federal law and deserves special study,
along with all the other state legislation which will control your
credit policy. Regulation Z applies to any individual or organization that "extends or arranges credit for which a finance charge is or may be payable or which is repayable by
agreement in more than four installments," but not to you if

Exhibit I. Nature of information disclosure.

Mr. Harry Doe
615 Avenue "B"
Anytown, USA

Dear Mr. Doe:

In response to your request for a statement of our reasons for turning down your recent application for credit, our records reveal that your application was not approved because:

> Your employer informed us that you were a part-time rather than full-time employee.

> or

> A department store in this city told us that you were several months behind on your payments.

> or

> The local branch office of a finance company informed us that it had turned your account with them over to a collection agency.

> or

> A bank in this city told us that your checking account was consistently overdrawn.

We appreciate your patronage, and invite you to shop with us on a cash basis.

Very truly yours,

Richard Roe,
Credit Manager

your customers unilaterally decide to pay your bills piecemeal. Nearly all kinds of credit are subject to the Regulation except these:

⇒ Commercial and business credit.
⇒ Credit to (but not from) federal, state and local governments.
⇒ Transactions in securities and commodities with broker-dealers who are registered with the Securities and Exchange Commission.
⇒ Non-real-estate credit over $25,000.
⇒ Agricultural credit transactions.

Apart from these exceptions, virtually all credit transactions require full disclosure of the true costs of credit. These are the obligations of any creditor complying with Regulation Z:

1   He must adopt the specific language and disclosure forms the Regulation prescribes.
2   He must maintain his credit records for at least two years.
3   He must state the annual percentage rate of finance charge to the nearest ¼ of 1 percent using the words "annual percentage rate."
4   He must disclose the full finance charge his customer pays for credit, including all these:
    Interest
    Any loan fee
    Any finder's fee
    Any time-price differential
    Any amount paid as a discount
    Any service, transaction or carrying charge
    Any "points," or prepaid interest
    Any investigation, credit report or appraisal fee in a non-real estate transaction
    The premium for credit-life, health, and accident insurance if it's a condition for giving credit

6•4
"OPEN-END" DISCLOSURES

Regulation Z divides credit into two categories and deals with each separately. The first is *open-end credit,* defined as any credit transaction in which a finance charge is added to the customer's unpaid balance each month. Most credit cards and revolving charge agreements are typical examples. You are obliged to provide all the following information before your customer's first open-end charge transaction takes place:

⇒ The conditions for imposing a finance charge and the period during which payment can be made without incurring a finance charge. Of course, you are always free to extend any grace period without notice.

⇒ The method used to determine the balance against which a finance charge will be imposed each month. You have a choice: consider the *previous balance* (outstanding for half the billing cycle), or use the *adjusted previous balance* (subtracting the payments made this month from the amount owed last month), or look at the *average daily balance* (adding each day's balance and dividing the total by the number of days in the cycle).

⇒ The way the actual finance charge is calculated.

⇒ The periodic rates used and the range of balance to which each applies.

⇒ The conditions under which any additional charges may be made and the way such charges would be calculated.

⇒ A description of any lien that may be acquired on a customer's property.

⇒ The minimum payment due each month.

⇒ A statement of the customer's rights to dispute billing errors under the Fair Credit Billing Act, substantially similar to the notice shown as Exhibit J.

After an account is opened, you must issue periodic statements if there is any finance charge imposed or if there is a debit or credit balance exceeding $1. These statements might

Exhibit J. Notice of billing error rights.

IN CASE OF ERRORS OR INQUIRIES ABOUT YOUR BILL

The Federal Truth in Lending Act requires prompt correction of billing mistakes.

1. *If you want to preserve your rights under the Act, here's what to do if you think your bill is wrong or if you need more information about an item on your bill:*
   (a) *Do not write on the bill. On a separate sheet of paper write* [**Alternate:** *Write on the bill or other sheet of paper*] *(you may telephone your inquiry but doing so will not preserve your rights under this law) the following:*
      i. *Your name and account number (if any).*
      ii. *A description of the error and an explanation (to the extent you can explain) why you believe it is an error.*
      If you only need more information, explain the item you are not sure about and, if you wish, ask for evidence of the charge such as a copy of the charge slip. Do not send in your copy of a sales slip or other document unless you have a duplicate copy for your records.
      iii. *The dollar amount of the suspected error.*
      iv. *Any other information (such as your address) which you think will help the creditor to identify you or the reason for your complaint or inquiry.*
   (b) *Send your billing error notice to the address on your bill which is listed after the words: "Send Inquiries To:" or similar wording.* [**Alternate:** *Send your billing error notice to: (creditor's name and address).*]
   Mail it as soon as you can, but in any case, early enough to reach the creditor within 60 days after the bill was mailed to you. If you have authorized your bank to automatically pay from your checking or savings account any credit card bills from that bank, you can stop or reverse payment on any amount you think is wrong by mailing your notice so the creditor receives it within 16 days after the bill was sent to you. However, you do not have to meet this 16-day deadline to get the creditor to investigate your billing error claim.

2. *The creditor must acknowledge all letters pointing out possible errors within 30 days of receipt, unless the creditor is able to correct your bill during that 30 days. Within 90 days after receiving your letter, the creditor must either correct the error or explain why the creditor believes the bill was correct. Once the creditor has explained the bill, the creditor has no further obligation to you even though you still believe that there is an error, except as provided in paragraph 5 below.*

3. *After the creditor has been notified, neither the creditor nor an attorney nor a collection agency may send you collection letters or take other collection action with respect to the amount in dispute; but periodic statements may be sent to you, and the disputed amount can be applied against your credit limit. You*

cannot be threatened with damage to your credit rating or sued for the amount in question, nor can the disputed amount be reported to a credit bureau or to other creditors as delinquent until the creditor has answered your inquiry. However, you remain obligated to pay the parts of your bill not in dispute.

4. *If it is determined that the creditor has made a mistake on your bill, you will not have to pay any finance charges on any disputed amount. If it turns out the creditor has not made an error, you may have to pay finance charges on the amount in dispute, and you will have to make up any missed minimum or required payments on the disputed amount. Unless you have agreed that your bill was correct, the creditor must send you a written notification of what you owe; and if it is determined that the creditor did make a mistake in billing the disputed amount, you must be given the time to pay which you normally are given to pay undisputed amounts before any more finance charges or late payment charges on the disputed amount can be charged to you.*

5. *If the creditor's explanation does not satisfy you and you notify the creditor **in writing** within **10** days after you receive his explanation that you still refuse to pay the disputed amount, the creditor may report you to credit bureaus and other creditors and may pursue regular collection procedures. But the creditor must also report that you think you do not owe the money, and the creditor must let you know to whom such reports were made. Once the matter has been settled between you and the creditor, the creditor must notify those to whom the creditor reported you as delinquent of the subsequent resolution.*

6. *If the creditor does not follow these rules, the creditor is not allowed to collect the first $50 of the disputed amount and finance charges, even if the bill turns out to be correct.*

7. *If you have a problem with property or services purchased with a credit card, you may have the right not to pay the remaining amount due on them, if you first try in good faith to return them or give the merchant a chance to correct the problem. There are two limitations on this right:*
   (a) You must have bought them in your home State or if not within your home State within 100 miles of your current mailing address; and
   (b) The purchase price must have been more than $50.
   However, these limitations do not apply if the merchant is owned or operated by the creditor, or if the creditor mailed you the advertisement for the property or services.

---

be similar to Exhibit K. Be sure to provide all the following information, to the extent applicable:

⇒ The debit or credit balance at the start of the billing period.

Exhibit K. A retailer's statement. Example of a retailer's statement, prepared by a manual billing operation, for an account on which the finance charge is determined by a single periodic rate or a minimum charge of 50 cents applicable to balances under a specific amount. It also assumes that the finance charge is computed on the previous balance before deducting payments and/or credits. Separate slips shall accompany each statement, identifying all charges and credits and showing the dates and amounts thereof.

Any Store U.S.A.

MAIN STREET—ANY CITY, U.S.A.

Direct customer inquiries to the attention of Mr. John Smith

(Customer's name here)

AMT. PAID $ _____

TO INSURE PROPER CREDIT RETURN THIS PORTION WITH YOUR PAYMENT

- -

PREVIOUS BALANCE	FINANCE CHARGE 50 CENTS MINIMUM	PAYMENTS	CREDITS	PURCHASES	NEW BALANCE	MINIMUM PAYMENT
	▲					

FINANCE CHARGE IS COMPUTED BY A "PERIODIC RATE" OF   % PER MONTH (OR A MINIMUM CHARGE OF 50 CENTS FOR BALANCES UNDER $) WHICH IS AN **ANNUAL PERCENTAGE RATE** OF   % APPLIED TO THE PREVIOUS BALANCE WITHOUT DEDUCTING CURRENT PAYMENTS AND/OR CREDITS APPEARING ON THIS STATEMENT.

NOTICE

PLEASE SEE ACCOMPANYING STATEMENT(S) FOR IMPORTANT INFORMATION.

▲

PAYMENTS, CREDITS OR CHARGES, RECEIVED AFTER THE DATE SHOWN ABOVE THE ARROW, WHICH IS THE CLOSING DATE OF THIS BILLING CYCLE, WILL APPEAR ON YOUR NEXT STATEMENT. TO AVOID ADDITIONAL FINANCE CHARGES PAY THE "NEW BALANCE" BEFORE THIS DATE NEXT MONTH.

ANY STORE, U.S.A. MAIN STREET, ANY CITY, U.S.A.

⇒ Copies of all sales vouchers or some other identification of each purchase transaction.

⇒ Dates and amounts of customer payments, and of any returns, credits or adjustments.

⇒ The finance charge in dollars and cents.

⇒ The rates used to compute the finance charge, plus the range of balances to which each rate applies.

⇒ The annual percentage rate: divide the finance charge by the unpaid balance to get the rate per month, then multiply the result by 12.

⇒ The actual unpaid balance used to calculate the finance charge.

⇒ The billing cycle's closing date and the balance at that time.

⇒ An address for customer inquiries.

⇒ A statement of the customer's rights under the Fair Credit Billing Act, unless you semiannually send the more comprehensive statement of rights in the event of a billing dispute. Your periodic statement might resemble Exhibit L.

6•5
TELLING ALL—ABOUT LOANS AND INSTALLMENT SALES

The second category includes all other credit transactions—loans, installment sales, and any extension of credit for a specified period, where the total amount and due dates are understood on Day One. They do not fall under the open-end rules and they require the following disclosures in writing before they are consummated:

⇒ The total finance charge in dollars and cents (except for transactions relating to dwellings).

⇒ The date the finance charge begins to accrue, if it's different from the date of the transaction.

⇒ The annual percentage rate (APR), unless the finance charge is less than $5 on credit under $75 or less than $7.50 on credit over $75. In calculating the annual percentage rate, payments must first be applied to interest and then to principal. APR tables are available from the Federal Reserve Board, its member banks, and various trade associations.

Exhibit L. Alternative to semiannual statement of billing error rights.

IN CASE OF ERRORS OR INQUIRIES ABOUT YOUR BILL

Send your inquiry in writing [**at creditor's option:** *on a separate sheet*] *so that the creditor receives it within 60 days after the bill was mailed to you. Your written inquiry must include:*

1. *Your name and account number (if any);*
2. *A description of the error and why (to the extent you can explain) you believe it is an error; and*
3. *The dollar amount of the suspected error.*

If you have authorized your creditor to automatically pay your bill from your checking or savings account, you can stop or reverse payment on any amount you think is wrong by mailing your notice so that the creditor receives it within 16 days after the bill was sent to you.

You remain obligated to pay the parts of your bill not in dispute, but you do not have to pay any amount in dispute during the time the creditor is resolving the dispute. During that same time, the creditor may not take any action to collect disputed amounts or report disputed amounts as delinquent.

If you have a problem with property or services purchased with a credit card, you may have the right not to pay the remaining amount due on them if you first try in good faith to return them or give the merchant a chance to correct the problem. There are two limitations on this right:

1. *You must have bought them in your home State or, if not within your home State, within 100 miles of your current mailing address; and*
2. *The purchase price must have been more than $50.*

However, these limitations do not apply if the merchant is owned or operated by the creditor, or if the creditor mailed you the advertisement for the property or services.

This is a summary of your rights; a full statement of your rights and the creditor's responsibilities under the Federal Fair Credit Billing Act will be sent to you both upon request and in response to a billing error notice.

⇒ The amounts and due dates of payments. Any irregular (or "balloon") payment must be included. If they are more than twice the amount of the regular payment, they must be labeled "balloon payments."

⇒ The total number of payments (except for first mortgages on dwellings).

⇒   The amount of any delinquency charge and how it would
    be calculated.
⇒   A description of any security you will hold.
⇒   The amount of any prepayment penalties.
⇒   A statement of the method used to compute the finance
    charge rebate in any contract calling for precomputed
    finance charges, along with an itemization of any charges
    to be deducted from the rebate.

Exhibit M tells the story the way you should.

6•6
THE SPECIAL LOAN DISCLOSURES
When the transaction is a *loan,* three more disclosures are in
order:

⇒   An itemized list of all items of credit. Include all charges
    beyond those that compose the finance charge, using the
    term "amount financed."
⇒   A statement of any amounts that are deducted as *prepaid*
    finance charge, and the required deposit balance.
⇒   The total finance charge with a description of each
    amount.

6•7
MORE ABOUT CREDIT SALES
A *credit sale* requires the following additional disclosures:

1 The cash price.
2 The down payment (including trade-ins).
3 The difference between the two, the so-called "unpaid balance of cash price."
4 An itemized list of all charges included in the amount financed, but not part of the finance charge.
5 The unpaid balance, the sum of (3) and (4).
6 Amounts deducted as prepaid finance charge or required
   deposit balances.

ANY STORE U.S.A.

Installment Loan Department

Account No. _____

DISCLOSURE STATEMENT OF SALE

Sale made this _____ day of _____, 19_____, to purchaser(s)

_____

Name(s)

_____

Address

by Seller (Creditor) _____ Name _____ Address

The Seller retains for itself and its assigns a security interest in the following property:

New/Used Year Make and Description Model Identification or Serial No.

_____

This security interest will secure all other indebtedness of Purchaser to Bank, including future loans and advances. The security interest extends to after acquired property affixed thereto.

(1) CASH PRICE _____ $_____

(2) LESS: CASH DOWN PAYMENT _____ $_____

(3)   TRADE IN _____ $_____

(3) (a) TOTAL DOWN PAYMENT _____ $_____

(4) UNPAID BALANCE OF CASH PRICE (1-3A) _____ $_____

(5) PROPERTY INSURANCE—The purchaser may choose the person through whom any property or liability insurance is to be obtained. If obtained through the creditor, the cost thereof is as follows:

Coverage _____ Total Property Insurance Premium _____ $_____

(6) PERSONAL INSURANCE—The following types of insurance are not required in connection with this transaction. The purchaser's desire for any such insurance must be indicated by signature below:

Credit Life Insurance   Premium $_____

_____
    Signature   Date
A & H Insurance   Premium $_____

_____
    Signature   Date
A.D. & D. Insurance   Premium $_____

_____
    Signature   Date

Total Personal Insurance Premium _____ $_____

(7) OTHER CHARGES: _____ $_____

(8) AMOUNT FINANCED (4 + 5 + 6 + 7) _____ $_____

(9) FINANCE CHARGE Time price differential _____ $_____

(10) TOTAL OF PAYMENTS (8 + 9) _____ $_____

(11) DEFERRED PAYMENT PRICE (1 + 5 + 6 + 7 + 9) $_____

(12) ANNUAL PERCENTAGE RATE _____%

(13) Item #10 payable in _____ monthly installments of $_____
each, beginning on _____, 19___ and continuing on the same
day of each month thereafter until paid with irregular payments,
if any, as follows:

_____

REBATE FOR PREPAYMENT IN FULL: If the contract is prepaid in full before the final installment date, the purchaser shall
receive a rebate of the unearned finance charges computed under
the Rule of 78's except that the bank shall retain a minimum charge
of $25.00.

DEFAULT CHARGE: In the event of default or late payment of
any installment, the purchaser agrees to pay a late charge in an
amount equal to five percent (5%) on each unpaid installment. If
legal action is necessary purchaser will be liable for costs of collection, including attorney's fees of 25%.

I acknowledge that I received a copy of this completed statement
before agreeing to purchase the above described property.

                          _____
                                    Purchaser

_____   _____
    Witness   Purchaser

7 The total amount financed, the difference between (5) and
(6).

8 Except for dwellings, the *deferred payment price* (the total of
the cash price, the finance charges and all other charges).

If you take telephone or mail orders, you can make these
additional disclosures any time before the first payment is
due, as long as the cash price, the down payment, the deferred payment price and the financing terms are made
known to the public first.

6 • 8
HOW REAL ESTATE CREDIT IS DIFFERENT
Real estate transactions follow the general rules for credit
sales, but are subject to special legislation. Note these
provisions in particular:

⇒   You need not show the total dollar amount of the finance
charge on a credit sale or first mortgage when the purchase is the customer's dwelling.

⇒   When the customer's residence is used as collateral for
credit (except for a first mortgage), he has the right to
cancel the transaction by letter or telegram within three
business days and get all his money back. This right may
be waived only under extraordinary circumstances, and
must be explained using the language shown in Exhibit N.

Exhibit N. Notice of right of rescission.

The form opposite is the form of notice of the right to rescind a
transaction required to be given to customers under certain circumstances
set forth in Section 226.9 of Regulation Z. Where the property on which
the security interest may arise does not include a dwelling, the creditor
may substitute the words "the property you are purchasing" for "your
home" or "lot" for "home" where these words appear in the form of
notice. This exhibit should be set in capital and lower case letters of
12 point bold faced type, the minimum size permissible under
Regulation Z.

(continued on next page)

Notice To Customer Required By Federal Law:

You have entered into a transaction on _____

which may result in a lien, mortgage, or other security interest on your home. You have a legal right under Federal law to cancel this transaction, if you desire to do so, without any penalty or obligation within three business days from the above date or any later date on which all material disclosures required under the Truth in Lending Act have been given to you. If you so cancel the transaction, any lien, mortgage, or other security interest on your home arising from this transaction is automatically void. You are also entitled to receive a refund of any downpayment or other consideration if you cancel. If you decide to cancel this transaction, you may do so by notifying.

_____

(Name of Creditor)

at _____

(Address of Creditor's Place of Business)

by mail or telegram sent not later than midnight of _____.
(Date)

You may also use any other form of written notice identifying the transaction if it is delivered to the above address not later than that time. This notice may be used for that purpose by dating and signing below.

I hereby cancel this transaction.

_____   _____
(Date)   (Customer's signature)

_____

(continued)

The following paragraph shall appear on the face or the reverse side of the notice shown on the preceding page. If it appears on the reverse side of the notice, the face of the notice shall state, "See reverse side for important information about your right of rescission."

EFFECT OF RESCISSION. When a customer exercises his right to rescind under paragraph (a) of this section, he is not liable for any finance or other charge, and any security interest becomes void upon such a rescission. Within 10 days after receipt of a notice of rescission, the creditor shall return to the customer any money or property given as earnest money, downpayment, or otherwise, and shall take any action necessary or appropriate to reflect the termination of any security interest created under the transaction. If the creditor has delivered any property to the customer, the customer may retain possession of it. Upon the performance of the creditor's obligations under this section, the customer shall tender the property to the creditor, except that if return of the property in kind would be impracticable or inequitable, the customer shall tender its reasonable value. Tender shall be made at the location of the property or at the residence of the customer, at the option of the customer. If the creditor does not take possession of the property within 10 days after tender by the customer, ownership of the property vests in the customer without obligation on his part to pay for it.

6•9
PLAYING YOUR CARDS RIGHT

There may be great appeal in sidestepping the problems of credit-risk evaluation and the billing and collecting process by using a nationally recognized credit-card program. The ease of prepackaged forms and the advertising advantage of the logo for Visa or Master Charge (or whatever) have forced many small-business owners to the same conclusion. The idea may well make sense for you. But before joining their ranks, consider the obligations you must undertake:

x   Your first obligation would be to pay a percentage of your monthly credit sales as the card company's fee, and to pay it promptly. The issuer would have the corresponding duty of billing and collecting for all valid card sales.

x   In addition, you might be asked to pay a nominal rental fee for use of the issuer's equipment. But expect all the proper forms to be free.

x   You would be forced to honor any valid card, so anticipate a big drop in cash sales. The issuer cannot, however, prevent you from offering a discount for cash sales.

x   You would be prohibited from honoring any suspicious cards, and called upon to inform the issuer of your suspicions.

x   You would be required to forward all sales slips and credit slips to the issuer within seven business days. After that, it's his responsibility.

x   Finally, you will be expected to indemnify the issuer from any claims resulting from defects in the goods you sell or in the services you render. (See section 6 • 12)

6 • 10
THE FORMS GAME

So the credit game is a forms game. The intelligent development and maintenance of your credit forms will assure your legal compliance as you expand into new markets from your existing customer base. Legal ends and business ends should merge, so that with the analytical capacity that a forms system inevitably fosters, you should reach a new high in controlling the targets of your sales, and, with that control, the collectability of your profit.

Work with your lawyer to develop a systematized approach to consumer-law compliance. Forms design and redesign will become a continuing, but worthwhile, demand as regulations—both federal and state—tighten and broaden. You should gain some additional knowledge of the way your business is affected right now by writing to the enforcement agency to which you are accountable. (You will find the address in Exhibit O.) Your lawyer will keep you abreast of changes in the law that might force you to alter the way you conduct your company's credit policy.

6 • 11
A COLLECTION PHILOSOPHY

However sophisticated your credit-evaluation procedure may be, a fraction of your receivables will prove difficult to collect. Bad receivables are an unavoidable cost of doing credit busi-

Exhibit O. Federal enforcement agencies.

From the list that follows, you will be able to tell which Federal agency covers your particular business. Any questions you have should be directed to that agency. These agencies are also responsible for enforcing Regulation Z.

NATIONAL BANKS

Comptroller of the Currency
United States Treasury
Department
Washington, D.C. 20220

STATE MEMBER BANKS

Federal Reserve Bank serving
the area in which the state
member bank is located.

NONMEMBER INSURED BANKS

Federal Deposit Insurance Corporation Supervising Examiner
for the District in which the
nonmember insured bank is
located.

SAVINGS INSTITUTIONS
INSURED BY THE FSLIC AND
MEMBERS OF THE FHLB
SYSTEM (EXCEPT FOR SAVINGS
BANKS INSURED BY FDIC)

The FHLBB's Supervisory Agent
in the Federal Home Loan Bank
District in which the institution
is located.

FEDERAL CREDIT UNIONS

Regional Office to the National
Credit Union Administration,
serving the area in which the
Federal Credit Union is located.

CREDITORS SUBJECT TO CIVIL
AERONAUTICS BOARD

Director, Bureau of Enforcement
Civil Aeronautics Board
1825 Connecticut Avenue, N.W.
Washington, D.C. 20428

CREDITORS SUBJECT TO
PACKERS AND STOCKYARDS
ACT

Nearest Packers and Stockyards
Administration area supervisor.

FEDERAL LAND BANKS,
FEDERAL LAND BANK
ASSOCIATIONS, FEDERAL
INTERMEDIATE CREDIT BANKS,
AND PRODUCTION CREDIT
ASSOCIATIONS

Farm Credit Administration
490 L'Enfant Plaza West
Washington, D.C. 20024

RETAIL DEPARTMENT STORES,
CONSUMER FINANCE
COMPANIES, ALL OTHER
CREDITORS, AND ALL
NONBANK CREDIT CARD
ISSUERS

Truth in Lending
Federal Trade Commission
Washington, D.C. 20580

ness, a cost well justified by the large majority of credit customers, who will meet their obligations to you without so much as a reminder.

Efficient credit management dictates the creation of still another system of forms, the strong and straightforward series of collection notices that will help turn receivables into cash. It is the notices' cumulative effect that will yield results. Don't be overzealous in your collection effort or you may unwittingly find yourself in violation of the law by overstating your collection message. Use restraint. Appeal to the debtor's sense of pride, fair play, and self-interest. Your integrity is far more valuable than any debt due you, so respect these FTC guidelines:

⇒ Avoid deceit. You're not seeking information in connection with a survey, and you don't have a prepaid package for the debtor. Disguising your purpose or holding out an inducement to debtors to furnish information they would not voluntarily furnish can only backfire.

⇒ Say who you are. Creating the impression that you are a government agency, a credit bureau, or a collection agency is forbidden, unless, of course, it's true.

⇒ Above all, refrain from threats.

Deceptive debt collection practices might give rise to lawsuits on grounds including libel, extortion, mental anguish, and invasion of privacy. Be straightforward but firm in your collection contacts. When all other attempts at collection fail, you may choose to exercise lawful "self-help" or refer the account to a reputable collection agency or, ultimately, to an attorney.

6•12
WHERE DUE PROCESS STOPS YOU

Due-process doctrines and consumer-oriented legislation place severe limitations on your recourses as a creditor. Be aware of these recent developments:

x Your unauthorized entry onto a debtor's premises for purposes of repossession is generally prohibited by the

Uniform Commercial Code as a "breach of the peace." And even though you may, for instance, repossess an automobile on a public road (if the debtor does not object) you may be held liable for any personal property within the car you repossess, and any protest by the debtor may preclude repossession altogether.

x   Any goods you do repossess will almost certainly need to be resold after notice to the debtor, at a "commercially reasonable" sale. Otherwise, you are subject to both damages and penalties.

x   You may not retain a "lay-away" deposit as liquidated damages after a customer's default; the practice has been labeled "unconscionable" by the courts.

x   You may not contractually place debt-collection jurisdiction in courts distant from the debtor. The Supreme Court has ruled that both the Uniform Commercial Code and the Federal Trade Commission Act prohibit this effective deprivation of justice.

x   Both prior notice to the debtor and a hearing are required for wage garnishments and for the *replevin* (that is, the recovery of possession) of household goods.

x   One of the FTC's newest promulgations severely limits the use of negotiable instruments and so-called "waiver-of-defense" clauses in consumer contracts.

Today, all consumer-credit contracts must clearly state in 10-point bold-face type:

> ANY HOLDER OF THIS CONSUMER CREDIT CONTRACT IS SUBJECT TO ALL CLAIMS AND DEFENSES WHICH THE DEBTOR COULD ASSERT AGAINST THE SELLER OF GOODS AND SERVICES OBTAINED PURSUANT HERETO OR WITH THE PROCEEDS HEREOF. RECOVERY HEREUNDER BY THE DEBTOR SHALL NOT EXCEED AMOUNTS PAID BY THE DEBTOR HEREUNDER.

A seller can no longer discount his customer's note to a finance company and be safe in the expectation that his customer will be forced to pay the finance company, even if the goods or services he sold prove defective. The finance company will be held responsible and will, in turn, hold the seller responsible.

Although the rule excludes credit card transactions, the Fair Credit Billing Act invalidates "waivers of defense" when purchases over $50 are made within a card user's state or within 100 miles of his residence.

6•13
COURT: THE LAST RESORT

Although self-help remedies are often valid alternatives to costly judicial process, your lawyer may offer the only practical recourse. Litigational approaches vary from state to state: you may proceed with a suit for money damages, a suit by confession on a promissory note, or a creditor's suit in a court of equity. After your day in court, supplementary proceedings can be instituted to collect on the judgment. These might include levying and executing on the debtor's property, or garnishing his wages or bank account.

No lawsuit is pleasant, and a lawsuit against a customer, past or present, is especially distasteful. The costs of litigation—in time, in money, in heartache—can best serve to underscore the importance of developing a sound and comprehensive credit policy at the outset, one that is destined for the highest degree of success.

7

LISTENING TO THE PROFESSIONALS

Courage is what it takes to stand up and speak; courage is also what it takes to sit down and listen.

—Winston Churchill

7•1
HOW THE PROFESSIONAL TEAM SHOULD WORK

It's undeniable. From the very start, you will need the help of the pros—the lawyer, the accountant, the banker and the insurance broker or agent. The only thing open to question is how you will use them. The less enlightened might contend that the professional's proper role is curative—the lawyer's, to bring or defend a lawsuit; the accountant's, to prepare those tax returns by the 15th; the banker's, to satisfy a sudden need for cash; and the broker's or agent's, to provide the policy you need to land that big contract.

The truth is that a business owner's exclusive reliance on after-the-fact, emergency advice can only work to his detriment. A professional's best contributions are preventive, steering you clear of costly mistakes and toward opportunities that you might otherwise miss.

Working as a team, united by a common interest in the growth and prosperity of your business, your business counselors can offer you the widest range of relevant knowledge and experience available anywhere. Even when their opinions conflict—and they will—the interaction among your advisers, each with his own professional bias, will help you isolate the issues and weigh the pros and cons intelligently.

7•2
MAKING GOOD USE OF YOUR LAWYER

Many small-business owners consult lawyers too seldom and too late. With the sheer volume and complexity of legal decisions you must face, your best bet is to consult your lawyer routinely. His input should prove indispensable in all these ways:

- ✔ *Reviews.* As soon as he is retained, a good lawyer will check your past course of action—your corporate minute book, existing contracts, leases and insurance policies, other live documents—and make recommendations. Thereafter, he will make periodic legal checkups.
- ✔ *Counseling.* Your lawyer will offer guidance whenever you seek it, and will initiate ideas on his own.
- ✔ *Information.* He can advise you in plain and simple English about the legality and efficacy of any action, and he should fill you in on the alternatives. What's more, it's his job to keep you abreast of changes in the laws that affect you, and the opportunities and pitfalls they carry.
- ✔ *Representation.* Of course, your lawyer will plead your case in court. Also count on him to represent your interests before government agencies, banks, other lawyers, anywhere he "speaks the language" better than you do.

7•3
WHAT A LAWYER IS SUPPOSED TO KNOW

More specifically, here are a few things any business lawyer who is worth his salt should be able to do for you:

- ✔ *Organization.* He will help you select the form of your business—corporation, partnership or whatever—and see to the mechanics.

✔ *Buying, selling, contracting, and leasing.* Negotiating your best deal may become your lawyer's responsibility, and he can spot the tax issues too.

✔ *Financing and credit.* He will shield you from the fine print in loan agreements and help you comply with all the new laws in this burgeoning area.

✔ *Taxes.* His eye will be toward the net-dollar amount in any transaction, and he will know how to maximize that amount even in light of the newest tax-reform legislation.

✔ *Complying with federal, state and local laws.* It is your lawyer's business to make you aware of the various pertinent laws and the easiest ways to conform to them.

✔ *Litigation.* Should a suit arise—or should you be forced to bring on—your lawyer (or his trial co-counsel) must be sharp enough and conversant enough with your business to tell your story to your best advantage.

7 • 4
THE QUEST FOR A GOOD LAWYER

Because of his uniquely diversified role, the lawyer can be critically important to your growth. Yet finding a lawyer who can make a difference in your business is a tough challenge. Forget about bar association referral services; they are helpful for individuals with consumer or domestic problems, for instance, but they can't be selective enough for business clients. And reject the advice of well-meaning friends who recommend their own lawyers; their needs are almost surely different from yours.

Other business owners in your general league are a good source of lawyer-leads. Their problems are apt to be similar to yours, and their success at solving them is worth your study. Non-lawyer professionals may also be helpful. They deal with business lawyers day in and day out, and can probably spot a conscientious one. More important, they will be privy to client comments, good and bad, and know who is satisfied with his lawyer and why. A final source of lawyer-

prospects is lawyers who are not seeking your account—
house lawyers for local companies, government lawyers, and
law school professors. These pros know other lawyers, can
judge competence, and may be purely objective.

Once you've got a few recommendations, the work begins
in earnest. Schedule an appointment with each prospect—
even though you may have to pay for his time—and have a
frank and full discussion. These are the things you will want
to know about:

⇒ *The size of his practice.* Even though a small firm can offer
   personalized attention, a large firm may have a broader
   range of expertise. Either way, satisfy yourself that the
   lawyer is not too busy to be accessible, and not so available that you can't help wondering why.
⇒ *His client base.* Find out if representing other small-
   business owners is a major part of his practice.
⇒ *His experience and specialty.* His background should qualify
   him to advise you on routine matters as well as on major
   decisions.
⇒ *His sounding board.* A cautious lawyer will consult other
   lawyers, both generalists and specialists, for your benefit.
   Find out whom he consults, and when.
⇒ *His philosophy.* You won't learn everything in one interview, but try to assess his basic attitudes toward the law
   and the conduct of business. It is important that his views
   be compatible with yours so that you can feel comfort-
   able in relying on his judgment.
⇒ *His style.* You will want a lawyer who can clearly, objec-
   tively, and logically present both sides of an issue. Avoid
   the highly opinionated, the pedantic, the overly glib, and
   the paternalistic.
⇒ *His fee structure.* Minimum fee schedules have been jet-
   tisoned, so you are left to informal comparisons and your
   own judgment of what is reasonable. Fees are a big
   source of attorney-client conflict, so discuss them openly
   at your first meeting.

7 • 5
WHAT PRICE ADVICE?

Here are some of the fee options:

A *retainer* is a periodic, fixed payment. What it buys can vary tremendously from lawyer to lawyer. Sometimes a retainer will entitle a client to unlimited telephone and office consultations and the review of routine documents. More often, a time limit is set, and exceeding it will trigger an invoice. Depending on the particulars, retainers may or may not make economic sense for you, but they will probably encourage freer use of your lawyer's time, and that's good.

An *hourly rate* is the most common, and often the fairest, method of payment. Be sure to ask for advance estimates, and don't be surprised if the hourly rate your lawyer quotes seems high: he's a small-business man too, whose fees must support his entire overhead.

Some routine matters may be charged at a *flat rate*. A simple employment agreement or a corporate resolution, for example, usually bears a fixed charge.

Collection cases and certain other matters can call for a *contingent fee*. Here, your lawyer is paid a negotiated percentage of any amount he recovers through settlement or at trial. He receives nothing if he recovers nothing. This is perhaps the only way a lawyer can be an entrepreneur within his own profession.

Sometimes, a *bonus fee*—beyond his regular billing—is awarded the lawyer who wins an important case or issue, but only if it's been agreed upon in front.

7 • 6
A CLIENT'S BILL OF RIGHTS

This is the age of consumerism. Once you have hired the lawyer who seems to meet your standards, take advantage of all your rights as a client:

- *Confidentiality.* It is your right to have your secrets and confidences preserved by any lawyer you consult.
- *Full information.* You have a right to learn all you want to learn about any pending legal matter, and that knowl-

edge should be communicated to you in language devoid
of legalese. This means that your lawyer must keep you
posted as to his progress in every matter he's handling
for you, . . . and in litigation he must pass along all bona
fide settlement offers as they are made. You also have a
right to receive copies of any documents, correspon-
dence, or pleadings prepared in your behalf.

✔ *Ultimate authority.* It is *your* problem-solving strategy that
you will use. So you—and not your lawyer—have a right
to decide which legal methods and objectives to pursue
and which to abandon. To this end, you have a right to
hear all sides of the issue, both from your lawyer and
from any other lawyer whose opinion you may solicit.

✔ *Reasonable fees.* As we have discussed, you and your lawyer
will reach agreement on his fee structure, and this agreement will become a contract binding on both of you. Insist on reasonable fees, set forth in frequent, itemized
bills.

✔ *Competence.* You have a right to loyal, skillful and energe-
tic representation by a lawyer who treats you courteously
and considerately.

✔ *Termination.* If all does not go well, you have a right to
call it quits upon payment of fair compensation for legal
services properly performed. Your lawyer will be obligated to respect your confidences and deliver your files
to your new lawyer.

7•7
HELPING YOURSELF

For your ultimate good, you have one more right—the right
to know what your lawyer expects of you. Hold up your side
of the bargain, and nurture a relationship that will work to
your absolute benefit. These are your obligations:

⇒ Avoid "freebies." Don't corner your lawyer on the golf
course to discuss your latest problem. Human nature
may force an off-the-cuff reaction that doesn't do you
justice. Instead, treat legal matters as serious business—

at your lawyer's office, on billable time, where together you can reach a deliberate, thoughtful solution.

⇒ Don't seek easy answers. Legal problems are often complex, so it is realistic to lower your sights and expect only competence, not miracles. Allow your lawyer the privilege of researching the law in depth and presenting the alternatives to you for discussion.

⇒ "Tell the truth, the whole truth, and nothing but." Don't withhold information and don't slant it. And notify your lawyer about changes in your business as they occur; he will be the judge of whether they are relevant to your legal decision making.

⇒ Finally, provide clear instructions. Always let your lawyer know what you want him to do so that he has a reasonable chance of meeting your expectations.

7•8
COUNTING ON YOUR ACCOUNTANT

In Chapter 3, we saw that accounting is not a science, but a descriptive art. It is not the mere application of a set of inflexible rules, but the deliberate selection of choices that bears heavily on the very vitality of your business. For this reason, the accountant, like the lawyer, should not be brought into the decision-making process in the eleventh hour, but in the first. In recruiting your accountant, consider these criteria:

✔ *A good reputation.* Your accountant must be familiar with and sympathetic toward the needs of small business. He will provide data which will influence your most significant business decisions, so he must be totally trustworthy and scrupulously honest.

✔ *Experience and skill.* Of course, your accountant must be competent. And, undoubtedly, the best accountant for you is one who really knows your type and size of operation and the ins and outs of its tax situation. The graduate accountant who passes a qualifying state test is a Certified Public Accountant. The CPA designation is itself an assurance of some knowledge and ability and is a requirement before an accountant can "certify" (legally guarantee) a financial statement.

✔ *Time and interest.* Your accountant must learn all sorts of facts about your business in order to create the best accounting system for you. If he lacks the time or motivation, the finished product will instead be prepackaged and generalized, so look elsewhere.

✔ *Service.* Your accountant will be asked to set up a system to provide all the information you truly need, no more and no less. Be sure his range of services will meet your requirements.

✔ *Reasonable fees.* "Cheap" is often no bargain, and "expensive" is only too much if it is more than you would need to pay to have work of the same quality done by another accountant.

7 • 9
THE ACCOUNTANT'S WORK PRODUCT

Your accountant's role is multifaceted. These are among the services he may provide:

✔ *Systematization.* He will create your accounting system and maintain it.

✔ *Review.* Through audits, he will periodically review the functioning of your system and recommend revisions in it as your business grows and changes.

✔ *Cost accounting.* He will trace profitability—and the lack of it—to nip profit-drainers in the bud.

✔ *Inventory and budget analyses.* He will help you see the forest among all those trees.

✔ *Tax management.* He may not advocate clever, illegal tax-avoidance schemes, but he should initiate important tax-saving moves which will (1) level peaks and valleys in the receipt of income, (2) accelerate or defer income and expense items, (3) divide income among related taxpayers, (4) convert high-taxed ordinary income into low-taxed capital gains, (5) build capital assets through legitimate R&D deductions and the 10 percent investment tax credit on certain capital assets purchased to upgrade the

productivity of your business, (6) use all the deductions
and exemptions available to you, and (7) save taxes
through appropriate ADR (section 3 • 7), fiscal-year (section 3 • 3), and other elections.

✔ *Assistance in raising capital.* He will prepare meaningful
financial statements for prospective investors, banks, and
other creditors, and may himself be a good source for
money contacts.

7•10
ACCOUNTING GOALS: PAST, PRESENT, AND FUTURE

The prime objective of accounting services is to provide information you can understand and use in these ways:

✔ *Evaluate the past.* Accounting is history. Your accountant
will study the hidden costs, tax liabilities, and unbalanced
inventories that hurt you last year and the year before so
that you can change your ways for the better in the year
to come.

✔ *Operate in the present.* Your accountant will provide the
day-to-day financial facts you need to operate and control your business.

✔ *Plan for the future.* Your accountant will chart the fore-
casts and projections that will form the basis of your future decisions, allowing you to budget your business resources with a minimum of waste and risk.

7•11
A PRO WITH SOMETHING TO SELL—YOUR BANKER

Your lawyer and accountant have nothing to sell but their
independent judgment. This is not the case with your insurance agent or broker, who peddles protection, or your
banker, whose stock-in-trade is cash. Nevertheless, for our
purposes, the insurance man (Chapter 8) and the banker are
professionals. They are expert and experienced business
counselors who play an important role in the success of virtually any venture.

It is usually not a banker that the businessman selects, but the bank where he works. Nevertheless, the banker's talent is tapped on the same personal basis as any other professional.

Ironically, you may choose your bank as you would any commercial (as opposed to professional) firm to perform services for you, on valid criteria like these:

⇒ *Services and location.* You may need a bank that offers specific services, like payroll processing or a night depository. And if a bank is geographically convenient to you, so much the better.

⇒ *Size.* You will want a bank big enough to fulfill your needs, now and in the future, yet not too big to take an interest in your growth.

⇒ *Reputation.* Your bank can be a major source of business contacts, and therefore you will want to enjoy the benefit of your bank's good relations with others in the community and elsewhere.

⇒ *General lending policy.* Loans are a bank's foremost product. You will want to know that the bank's lending policy will not exclude you, and, for example, whether it extends letters of credit to small-business owners, or short-term loans on accounts receivable or warehouse receipts.

7•12
BANKING ON YOUR BANK

On closer analysis, a bank must meet the same expectations you have for any professional. The bank's management philosophy, a philosophy manifested in its attitudes and policies, must dovetail with your needs before a banker may be added to your professional team. Interview your banker just as you would any pro, and satisfy yourself:

✔ *Is he interested in your business?* The bank that's on your side has declared itself in favor of the small business. And the banker for you is one who is eager to grow with your business.

✔ *Is he familiar with your type of business?* A banker's knowledge of a business can go a long way toward offsetting his natural conservatism. And his experience and insight can prove to be valuable resources for you.

↳ *Is he progressive?* Without question, you will need a bank that extends credit to people in your position at a reasonable rate of interest. One test: if all the bank's assets are in readily liquidated securities, management is probably very conservative and tough on loans.

↳ *How much help is he willing to offer?* When a bank cannot lend you money, it should be able to find someone who can, such as a bank-owned Small Business Investment Company (SBIC) (section 11•3) or another venture-capital source. A bank should also be willing to provide you with credit information on customers and suppliers. And it should want to make operating recommendations to help you grow successfully.

7•13
CASHING IN

Once you have found a banker you can count on, start at once to build a productive relationship. The more he knows about you and cares about you, the more valuable he will become as a player on your professional team. And, wearing his money-seller's hat, he will eventually be more receptive to a loan request.

Visit your banker frequently and keep him fully and candidly informed about your business. He will be glad to receive all the hard information you care to share with him—annual financials, budgets, anything that helps tell your story. Demonstrate your confidence in the future, but acknowledge any business shortcomings too. Your banker, who may well know about any problems before you reveal them, will appreciate your honesty and astuteness. And he will welcome the opportunity to offer the advice that you just might need. What's more, you will be bolstering your banker's faith in your good character, a wise investment against the day you really need money.

Surprisingly, bankers are very reluctant to lend money to those who urgently need it. A strong, durable relationship with your banker can guard against an abrupt turndown.

Whenever you're after a bank loan, adopt this bargaining posture:

1   The image you project is critically important. Since everyone loves a winner, come on like one. Hide any feelings of desperation. And act as if there is no doubt about your eligibility for a loan: the only purpose for your meeting is to agree on its terms.

2   Back up your "confidence" with all the detailed data you can muster. Bankers love facts and figures, so submit recent balance sheets, profit-and-loss statements, sales and profit projections (contemplating the use of loan proceeds and their payback), personal financials. And put a ribbon on the package with positive research summaries and favorable publicity.

3   Don't hide the negatives; they'll be discovered, anyway. Lay all your cards out and, as best you can, explain the missing aces.

4   Know what you want and shoot for it:

—A *line of credit* is an open-ended agreement by the bank to provide short-term credit up to a certain amount and under certain conditions. It is usually for seasonal and discount purposes rather than capital investment, and is a convenient way to firm up credit needs in advance.

—A *short-term loan* has a term of one year or less, and is also for working capital purposes, usually to take advantage of discounts. Some banks require a minimum deposit of 10 to 20 percent of the loan proceeds, effectively reducing available borrowed funds.

— An *intermediate-term loan* may be for working-capital purposes too, or it may be an alternative to equity financing. Security or collateral may be real estate, securities, life insurance policies, equipment, accounts receivable, or warehouse receipts.

— A *long-term loan* is generally unavailable from a bank except for real estate financing.

—*Equity financing* is not readily available directly from a bank, either, since its investments are highly regulated. Many banks do own SBICs and thus can provide access to venture capital; and, of course, banks do recommend investment opportunities to their select customers. (See section 11 • 2).

5 Negotiate for a loan as you would for anything else. Ask for more than you need so you can maintain a fall-back position. And avoid off-the-cuff answers to hard questions. You can always defer to your lawyer, your partner, or your board, and can, with the benefit of time to plot a course, come back with a well-conceived counterattack.

6 Don't be blinded by the appearance of success. Getting a loan is not your purpose; getting the loan you need—with a reasonable interest rate, over a reasonable term, with only reasonable strings attached—is.

7•14
TEAMING UP

The lawyer, the accountant, the insurance agent or broker, and the banker are your professional team. Each must offer advice from his own vantage point, advice which may or may not be in harmony with that of the others. But each offers the access to the outside world upon which your business will feed.

8

PROTECTING YOURSELF

The time will come when human intelligence will rise to the mastery of property.

—Lewis Henry Morgan

8 • 1
THE BEST MAN

Every business is exposed to obvious and not-so-obvious risks, risks that can cost big money and, at worst, can stymie future growth. Guard against those bleak possibilities by taking a conservative approach to protect your business as well as possible.

An affirmative risk-management program should be developed with the counsel of a competent insurance agent or broker, one familiar with your needs and the peculiarities of the insurance marketplace. Choose your agent carefully, as you would any professional, and count on him for these services:

- ✔ A thorough insurance-oriented evaluation of your present and proposed business operations.
- ✔ A careful comparison of insurance alternatives.
- ✔ Negotiation of contracts for coverage where your needs justify a special word on your behalf.
- ✔ Administrative help in the establishment of simplified procedures within your business to handle necessary insurance paperwork.

✔ Sound advice on loss prevention.
✔ Guidance in your compliance with the Occupational Safety and Health Act (sections 9 • 6 and 9 • 7) and the Environmental Protection Act.
✔ Assistance in claims processing.
✔ An annual review of your insurance program.

Every insurance agent will boast of access to financially stable insurance companies that offer the least expensive coverage and the fastest claims service available anywhere. The truth is that brokers and agents are salesmen, and while most are reputable and sincere, all of them are looking to you and others like you to pay their rent. So buy your insurance cautiously, from someone you know to be responsible and knowledgeable.

8 • 2
THE PRINCIPAL PRINCIPLES

Finding a good insurance agent is only the beginning of your insurance planning. Granted, with its own jargon and its own legal rules, insurance is a bewildering concept for most laymen, and most of us would rather leave insurance planning entirely to others. But sound business management demands your continuing control. With a firm grasp on a few basic principles and with the aid of an agent you can trust, your decision making in insurance matters is bound to improve:

⇒ An *insurance policy* is simply a contract by which the insurance company or *carrier* undertakes the risk of paying out a dollar amount, or *benefit,* upon the occurrence of an unlikely event (usually a casualty). In exchange, you agree to pay a fee, or *premium,* for the carrier's assumption of this risk. The policy describes what is covered, when, and to what extent, and your lawyer should study it carefully. It may also set out all kinds of procedures: how to file a claim, how to cancel coverage, how to assign your benefits, and even how to order more coverage.

⇒ The basic policy may be amended, or *endorsed,* at the outset or later on. Endorsements can be used to extend coverage to the particular risks of your business or locale. Or they can be used to exclude unnecessary or separately insured perils, thereby lowering the premium. Special policies (on boilers or plate glass, for example) allow the deletion of these risks from general coverage, and thus reduce insurance costs.

⇒ Insurance policies can be *specific* or *blanket.* A specific policy identifies, or *schedules* each item of insured property, locates it, and assigns a value to it. (Scheduling a valuable piece of equipment or an art object establishes its worth in front.) A blanket policy may offer greater flexibility in claims settlement by assigning value to insured property as a lot; a recovery limit is not set for any individual item, just for the aggregate.

⇒ A *package policy* insures multiple risks in a single, comprehensive contract. When similar risks are packaged and insured together, gapping and overlapping coverage can successfully be avoided, and so can disputes between carriers. On the other hand, the packaging of dissimilar risks might deprive you of the broader coverage individual policies would offer and will surely complicate your comparative analysis of competing policies.

⇒ If there are wide fluctuations in the value of your inventory or other insurable assets, *reporting insurance* may be more economical for you. Unlike other insurance premiums, which are usually based on the value of insured property when purchased, reporting-insurance premiums and coverage can rise and fall with your periodic reports of asset holdings.

⇒ The actual payout upon a loss can be the *actual cash value* (the cost less true physical depreciation) or *actual replacement cost.* These standards differ dramatically, so note which value the company elects in any policy you are reviewing. And spot whether an adjustment is made in instances where insured items have a far greater value than their replacement costs; blueprints, manuscripts, microfilm, and computer software are good examples.

⇒   The payout will be reduced if you fail to keep your part of the bargain described in a *co-insurance clause* (alias the *average clause,* the *percentage-of-value clause,* or the *contribution clause*). The co-insurance clause is used by carriers to keep insurance costs down by preventing selective underinsuring. It works like this: the insured agrees to buy coverage for, let's say, at least 80 percent of his property's value. The payout is limited by the percentage of any deficit in coverage. An insured who is obliged to maintain 80 percent (or $80,000 coverage on $100,000 property), but who carries only a $40,000 policy, will find his benefit cut in half at the time of loss. As property appreciates in value, the co-insurance clause calls for additional insurance purchases, so frequent reappraisals are a good idea.

⇒   A *deductible*—the first dollars of loss, those that become your expense and not the carrier's—is a big premium saver. With a deductible, the benefits you buy can be limited to a percentage of a loss, can start at a specific dollar level, or can commence after the passage of a fixed loss-time period. A variation is the *disappearing deductible,* which gradually diminishes as a loss increases. For expected mini-losses or really remote maxi-losses, opt for the largest deductible you can reasonably afford, and your insurance costs should plummet.

8 • 3
AN INSURANCE STRATEGY

The partial listing of the insurance policies available to you (Exhibit P) attests to the staggering complexity of insurance-purchasing decisions. Rely on an agent or broker who is more than a salesman, and systematically evaluate your insurance needs. Follow these rules and you can avoid both underinsurance and overinsurance:

1   Pinpoint your legal liability—on contracts, leases, deliveries, all transactions—and consider covering your exposure.

Exhibit P. A catalog of popular insurance products.

Accounts receivable insurance
Automobile insurance . . .
  liability, collision, comprehensive, medical payments, uninsured motorists' protection, and coverage on non-owned autos
Bailee's customers insurance
Blanket contractual coverage
Boiler insurance
Broad-form property-damage insurance
Business interruption insurance
Comprehensive general liability insurance
Credit insurance
Disability insurance
Dishonesty, disappearance, and destruction coverage
Earthquake insurance
Employee's liability insurance
Fire insurance . . . with extended coverage, special "all risk" extended coverage, and sprinkler damage coverage
Flood insurance
Forgery insurance
Inland transit insurance
Key-man life insurance
Leasehold insurance
Machinery and equipment insurance
Marine transit insurance
Medical–dental–surgical insurance
Occupational disease coverage
Owner's, landlord's and tenant's insurance
Partnership buy-sell funding
Payroll insurance
Plate glass insurance
Product liability insurance
Profits and commissions coverage
Public liability insurance
Rent insurance
Salesman's samples insurance
Security and theft insurance . . . including robbery, safe, and alarm system insurance
Shareholder buy-sell funding
Sole proprietorship life insurance
Surety bonds for employees
Umbrella liability coverage
Valuable papers and documents insurance
Vandalism and malicious mischief coverage
Workmen's compensation coverage

2 Assess nontransactional risks too, such as any valuable artwork in your executive offices.

3 Evaluate your overall susceptibility to business interruptions, whether from a fire, a machine breakdown, the loss of a key employee or supplier, or in the transportation network that supports you.

4   Forecast your product liability to consumers, other users, and even nonusers. And remember that your implied and express warranties (section 5•3) may be ripe for insurance backup.

5   Once you have translated all this vulnerability into a dollar projection, back off: only a tiny fraction of the risks your business faces is insurable. Your insurance professional will sort out what you can insure from what you cannot, including the biggest risk of all, the risk of plain old mismanagement.

6   After you have learned what is insurable, forget all the inconsequential risks you really don't need to cover; insuring against predictable small losses is usually an expensive nuisance.

7   Finally, forget about insuring any risk you can deal with in some other way at less cost and effort. More on this cost-justification idea later, when "self-insurance" is considered. (See section 8•8)

8   One footnote: Don't let your purchase of all the coverage you need and can afford conclude your insurance planning. Even for the insured, any loss is, at best, an inconvenience; at worst, a disaster. Loss prevention, with the guidance of a professional, is central to enlightened risk management.

8 • 4
READING THE "FINE PRINT"

All your well-intentioned insurance planning will prove ineffective if you take insurance at face value. Insurance companies exist to make money and, to that end, have earned a well-deserved reputation for "fine printing." With the help of your independent agent or broker, you can guard against hearing bad news like this, when it may be too late:

x   *"You have no insurable interest."* Unless you would suffer a direct financial loss from the insured property's damage or destruction, don't ever expect a payout. A few policies will even demand your sole and unconditional ownership before policy benefits attach. Be certain to inform the carrier of your ownership interest at the time of your insurance purchase and of any changes as they occur.

x *"You breached your warranty (or representation)."* Your application for coverage will elicit *warranties,* facts you guarantee to be true, and *representations,* assertions the carrier has a right to rely on. Any warranty or material representation that proves false might result in having your policy voided retroactively. So shun even a "white lie."

x *"The policy was never formally assigned to you."* While accrued insurance proceeds are assignable without carrier permission, policies themselves cannot be assigned without the insurance company's consent. When buying insured property, make certain that contractual-assignment provisions are fully observed, or obtain new coverage.

x *"The insurance company is not bound."* Where a standard insurance contract and its endorsement conflict, the endorsement governs. Your broker's opinion about a policy's true intent will not be binding on anybody, so if there is ambiguity, get written clarification from the carrier. By the same token, your letter to a broker, detailing changes in relevant facts or circumstances, won't constitute legal notice to the carrier unless the broker happens to be an agent of the carrier. Insist on acknowledgment by the insurance company.

x *"You violated the policy."* Your violation of a policy term or condition will usually suspend coverage until the violation is corrected. In a few states, however, coverage will remain suspended until specifically reinstated by the insurance company. Be safe; after any violation is remedied, ask for written confirmation that coverage has resumed.

x *"You have double coverage."* Buying a second policy on insured property requires the consent of the first carrier or endorsement for additional insurance on the first contract. Even if these requirements are met, you can never collect more than the insured property's value; the two carriers on the hook would each pay a pro rata share of the loss.

8 • 5
PROTECTING YOUR PROPERTY

Now let's look at your *property* insurance needs as your broker or agent might. Property coverage insures your business assets against all the risks you can think of, and then some:

⇒ The basic *fire* policy is usually extended to cover direct damage from smoke, wind, hail, riots, aircraft, and most explosions. But don't feel too secure: only stated risks are insured. You should consider endorsements to protect against *supplemental perils* (such as sprinkler damage, vandalism, and malicious mischief) and *climatic perils* (such as earthquakes and tornadoes). And bear in mind that the loss of money and securities, and even the loss of business, is simply not considered in the standard fire policy.

⇒ *Crime* policies may be necessary to the survival of your business. Where the risk of loss by crime is exceptionally high, you may turn to subsidized Federal Crime Insurance. But whatever the source, consider *burglary* coverage, affording protection against forced entries; *theft* coverage, covering disappearances without evidence of forced entry; and *robbery* coverage, insuring against losses by force, threats, or trickery on or off your premises. You can supplement these "external" crime coverages with "internal" insurance protection against *forgery,* and *fidelity bond* protection against employee dishonesty. Or package your crime insurance in a comprehensive *dishonesty, disappearance, and destruction* policy, and you will be safeguarded against employee thefts too.

⇒ *Floater* and *transit* policies cover personal property against fire and casualty. Whereas a floater insures goods wherever they may be, a transit policy covers them only from a specific point of departure to a specific point of arrival.

A word about floaters: *Salesmen's samples* are excluded from automobile policies, so insure them separately. And goods you're holding for others deserve *bailee's customers* insurance.

Remember your transit insurance needs too. *Inland transit* policies, including special parcel post insurance and rail transport insurance, can be limited or broad, and are often keyed to particular bill-of-lading forms. *Marine transit* coverage is usually sold on an all-risk, warehouse-to-warehouse basis and can be purchased at low cost by businesses complying with rigid packaging and shipping standards.

8 • 6
DON'T SUFFER THE CONSEQUENCES

Property coverage will compensate you only for the value of a damaged or destroyed asset. *Indirect-and-consequential* coverage, in all its forms, looks to the more far-reaching economic ramifications of property loss:

⇒ If your business property is damaged or destroyed, *business interruption* insurance can restore your lost profits and reimburse you for ongoing operational and recovery expenses, even for the expenses of moving to temporary quarters. Your policy can be endorsed to protect you against so-called *contingent interruptions* such as a power failure or a business interruption suffered by a major supplier.

⇒ *Rent* insurance covers the reduction or loss of income resulting from damage to rental property.

⇒ *Leasehold* insurance covers the value of improvements to leased property when damage causes the cancellation of a lease.

⇒ *Accounts receivable* insurance covers the cost of reconstructing damaged or destroyed receivable ledgers and supporting documentation and is thus an alternative to maintaining duplicate records off-premises. It can even compensate you for collections lost in the interim.

⇒ *Credit* insurance can protect you against the contingency of customer bankruptcy. This coverage is designed to lessen the impact of an extraordinary insolvency. A high deductible would meet or exceed a reasonable allowance for usual bad debts. In the foreign marketplace, buy an *insolvency-and-political-risk* policy from the Foreign Credit Insurance Association or the Import-Export Bank.

⇒ *Profits and commissions* coverage protects the commission of
    a seller whose income depends on a manufacturer's ability
    to supply a product.

8•7
DO UNTO OTHERS . . .

Liability insurance protects your business against the claims of
others who sustain personal injury or property damage for
which you are legally responsible. Courts are continually en-
larging the scope of your legal liability to others, and damage
awards relentlessly grow larger year by year. Apart from a
comprehensive *general liability* policy, specialized policies will
satisfy your liability needs, including these:

⇒ *Workmen's compensation* and *occupational disease* coverage,
    possibly mandatory in your state, will discharge your lia-
    bility to employees for job-related injuries or diseases, lia-
    bility that is yours even though you may not be negligent.
    Those employees who are permissively excluded from
    coverage can be protected under *employer's liability* insur-
    ance. Both workmen's comp and employer's liability
    should be carefully integrated with *disability* insurance (to
    reimburse an employee's salary or part of it when work-
    men's comp benefits do not apply) and with any disability
    provisions in your retirement plan.
⇒ "No-fault" auto insurance plans are progressively re-
    defining needs in the critical auto liability area. Such plans
    prescribe immediate payments to passengers in insured
    vehicles for lost wages and actual expenses, without re-
    gard to fault; pain-and-suffering damages are limited by
    statute. Where "no-fault" has not yet been enacted, *auto
    liability* coverage is often required by law, and is always a
    necessity.
        You are protected if your business vehicle causes an
    accident resulting in personal injury or property damage.
    Policy limits run from $10,000 to $100,000 for each per-
    son injured or killed, from $20,000 to $300,000 for the
    total of injuries and deaths sustained in the same accident,
    and $5,000 or more for property damage. Tort law may

hold a business liable for auto accidents caused by its employees, even when they're driving their own vehicles, so buy *non-owned auto* coverage and contractually bind your employees to maintain adequate coverage on their own cars.

Liability coverage is often packaged with other kinds of protection, such as (1) *collision* protection, which pays for damage to your vehicles (less a deductible of at least $100) even if you or your employee were to blame, (2) *comprehensive* coverage, which guards against non-collision damage (including fire and theft, on a deductible or actual-cash-value basis), (3) medical payments for passengers of your vehicles (generally up to $5,000), and (4) *uninsured motorist's* protection, which insures the passengers of your vehicles against injury caused by a driver without liability coverage.

⇒ *Product liability* coverage is costly and increasingly hard to get, but it's indispensable to many businesses. In recent years, courts throughout the nation have declared that one who manufactures or markets a product that is found to be "unreasonably dangerous" is responsible for injuries that result from use of the product, even if there is no negligence involved. The manufacturer is deemed an expert, and he, not the injured consumer, is thought to be in the best position to bear the risk of accidental injury. The theory applies even to a wholesaler who sells a packaged product that passes through his warehouse unopened.

Product liability judgments running into the millions are no longer a rarity. The industry was aroused at a seminar convened by the Society of Chartered Property and Casualty Underwriters in early 1976 in Tampa, Florida. John M. Haker of Northwestern National Insurance Company cited the kinds of products most likely to generate liability claims:

> Those used in dangerous occupations [for example, by] steeplejacks [and] deep-sea divers . . . involve a high degree of risk. The equipment they use is involved in this exposure. Ladders, ropes, scaffolding . . . are asso-

ciated with very severe injuries. This association makes such products very difficult to write, even though the product may be well-engineered.

You have only to look at the Consumer Product Safety Commission list of products most frequently involved in accidents. Bicycles, swing sets, ladders, and power mowers rank high on the list of products associated with frequent injuries. . . . If your product injures people, you will probably have to pay.

Those which involve particularly large potential loss. . . aircraft parts, for example, can result in losses into the tens of millions. Those involving batch exposures [such as] an animal feed loss [that] affected thousands of cattle. . . . Those products used in delicate medical treatment [such as] oxygen equipment, kidney dialysis equipment. . . .

Those items whose final usage is difficult to determine. . . . Foreign made products. . .

With more and more insurance carriers pulling out of the now unprofitable products-liability market, finding coverage may itself be troublesome, but, especially for target manufacturers and distributors, it is absolutely imperative. (See section 5 • 3)

⇒ *Umbrella liability* coverage, a relatively new policy, covers excess claims over and above the limits of other liability policies, including your general liability policy. Intended to cover only extraordinary claims, umbrella coverage is usually written with a large deductible and lets you purchase your other liability policies at lesser limits with smaller premiums.

8 • 8
SELF-INSURANCE: DOING IT YOURSELF

With so much expense and sometimes so little to show for it, more and more businesses are deciding to bear the risk of certain kinds of loss internally. The concept is neither novel nor outlandish: deductibles and uninsured risks in "named peril" policies always create self-insurance exposure for businesses.

Risk retention should never be a negligent default in planning. It can be a deliberate and positive way of reducing overall costs and enhancing cash flow when losses are predictable or when insurance costs are prohibitively high.

Self-insurance must be a rational program geared to your enterprise's fiscal condition, and not a simpleminded jump at front-end cost savings. Some businesses limit their self-insurance exposure to 5 percent or less of their net working capital; others set a maximum of 1 percent of average pretax earnings over the last five years. Your attorney can work with your accountant to develop a conservative risk profile for your enterprise.

In general, any good self-insurance program is a product of the kinds of risks that are retained. Small property-damage exposure, for instance, probably needs little or no formal structuring: as losses occur they are merely charged against an operating budget. If a business has the working capital and management orientation to retain major risks, it will ordinarily set up a loss reserve, either on paper or actually funded, with the premium that otherwise would be used to pay an insurer. If the retained risk is a deductible, the loss reserve amounts to the difference between the cost of coverage from the first dollar and the premium actually paid.

As a self-insurer, you will eventually try to accumulate at least twice as much as you might lose in a single occurrence. In the meantime, prepare to finance your retained risk by making a one-time, start-up contribution, by slowly phasing into self-insurance until the fund can hold its own, or by arranging standby bank loans capable of a quick drawdown at current interest rates.

Although your reserve might be an expensive undertaking, (especially since it may be ineligible for tax deductions except when losses are incurred), it can become a source of income through investment rather than an insurance-premium drain. And loss control may well be improved: when each profit center bears the risk of its own losses, managers will diligently strengthen their safety and security precautions.

One way to start retaining risks is to opt for large-scale deductibles where straight-dollar amounts are excluded from each loss payout. The amount of retained loss can be fixed, and the balance can be insured with carriers offering claims management and loss control services.

Another way to combine self-insurance with classical policy purchases is *retrospective rating.* Retrospective rating is popular in general liability and in auto and workmen's comp lines (where allowed by law) and is particularly useful where a business anticipates a marked improvement in its claims experience.

Retrospective rating works this way:

You pay your insurer a basic premium to approximate the cost of administering your program, including the adjustment of your claims. Your also pay an *excess loss* (catastrophe) premium to buy insurance on claims over a predetermined self-insurance limit. The total of actual losses for a one-year term is multiplied by a *loss-conversion factor* to establish the insurer's actual fee for handling claims.

Retrospective rating is one innovative way of fixing an income floor for the insurer and an expense ceiling for the insured. Risk retention, whether through retrospective rating or any of a stunning variety of other imaginative approaches, is surely not desirable for every business; legal, inspection, and administrative expenses alone will restrict some to traditional insuring. Yet everyone should have an open mind to the dynamic opportunities of insurance. With the aid of a top-notch insurance adviser and, of course, your attorney, relate your risk-management needs to the financial position and objectives of your business.

9

RELATING TO THE RANK AND FILE

Labor is the superior of capital, and deserves much the higher consideration.

—Abraham Lincoln

9 • 1
YOUR GOALS AND THEIRS

Good employee relations do not spring like a phoenix from the ashes of a union organizer's cigar; they grow over time in businesses that adopt personnel policies that are sound, employee-directed, and yet cost-effective. Maintaining high standards in the following areas will pay off in terms of a stable, remunerative workforce:

✔ *Security.* Be neither arbitrary nor discriminatory in hiring, firing and promoting. And underscore your concern with a solid health-and-welfare program.

✔ *Fairness.* Create a merit system based on objective job evaluations, and offer the dedicated employee: (1) the income he needs to maintain his standard of living, (2) a reasonable opportunity to build his net worth, (3) a cushion against any catastrophe that might befall him, (4) an allowance for his retirement, and (5) a hedge against infla-

tion. And encourage your employees to voice their real
complaints.

✔ *Good working conditions.* Physically, this means a safe and
decent place to work. Psychologically, it means a suppor-
tive environment of acceptance, dignity, and respect.

✔ *Humanity.* Your strong interest in your employees' well-
being will inspire them. And the sense of participatory
responsibility and accomplishment you instill in them will
mature into a loyalty that's all to your benefit.

9 • 2
THE FEDERAL LAW

These nondiscriminatory business objectives conform neatly
to legal requirements. Equal employment opportunity, for
example, is guaranteed by Title VII of the 1964 Civil Rights
Act. The Act prohibits discrimination in employment on the
basis of race, creed, color, sex, or national origin by all employers of 15 or more persons, and by all educational institutions, employment agencies, state and local governments, and
labor-management committees for training. Other laws have
expanded Title VII's scope and enlarged the enforcement
powers of both the federal and state governments:

⇒ The Equal Employment Opportunity Act gives the Equal
    Employment Opportunity Commission (EEOC) power to
    sue for the kinds of discrimination outlawed by Title VII.

⇒ The Equal Pay Act, a part of the Fair Labor Standards
    Act, demands equal pay to men and women for equal
    work.

⇒ The Age Discrimination Act prohibits discrimination on
    the basis of age, particularly benefiting those between the
    ages of 40 and 65.

⇒ The National Labor Relations Act bans both internal and
    external discrimination by unions, and it prohibits em-
    ployers from discriminating on the basis of union mem-
    bership or nonmembership.

⇒ And some state laws set even higher standards than these
    federal laws do.

9 • 3
EQUAL EMPLOYMENT OPPORTUNITY

Title VII and the EEO amendments prohibit discrimination in hiring and firing, and in promotions, privileges, compensation and conditions of employment. The only exceptions lie in "bona fide occupational qualifications," which are rare indeed. Watch out for these compliance pitfalls:

x   Don't advertise for a "girl Friday" (that's sexist) or a "recent college grad" (that's age-discriminatory).

x   Avoid the third degree on employment applications. Even seemingly harmless informational questions have been held discriminatory by the EEOC. Asking an applicant's place of birth, hair or eye color, and even height and weight are challengeable as discrimination by race or national origin.

Inquiry about marital status can be discriminatory. And asking one's age is not permitted, unless the application form acknowledges that discrimination on the basis of age is illegal.

Bringing an applicant's educational background into question can constitute a violation too. Requiring a high school diploma, for example, has been held to discriminate against minorities in employment situations where graduation need not rationally be a requirement for a specific job.

Even credit ratings and arrest records (but not conviction records) are improper areas of inquiry; they have been held to discriminate unfairly against minorities.

x   Try to eliminate subjective evaluations throughout the hiring process. Co-worker preference and traditional role stereotypes are totally unacceptable recruitment criteria.

x   It may be best to omit employment and promotion testing altogether. So many tests have been held discriminatory against undereducated and foreign-born minorities that their validity—and legality—are highly doubtful. Any tests you do adopt should first be validated as both job-related and nondiscriminatory.

x It is illegal to limit fringe benefits to "heads of household" or "principal wage earners" or to exclude husbands of female workers if wives of male workers are benefited. Pregnancy and childbirth must be treated as any other temporary disability. And the additional cost of providing these benefits to females is no defense to their omission.

x Never fire anyone without giving him the courtesy of an exit interview where he can learn the specific reasons for your decision. Be specific: personnel-file notations such as "He can't get along with co-workers" or "He received an adverse supervisor report" have given rise to covert discrimination charges.

9 • 4
THE EEOC AND YOU

Title VII and the EEO amendments are enforced by the EEOC and its enforcement powers are considerable. Employers of over 100 employees are automatically monitored by the Commission, since they are obliged to file periodic informational reports. Other employers subject to the Act (not everyone is) are scrutinized only after a complaint is filed by anyone within 180 days of an alleged violation.

Upon receiving a complaint, the EEOC will send a copy of it along with form interrogatories to the respondent-employer. The employer's answers to interrogatories, prepared under a lawyer's direction, may be the only input the Commission will consider on his behalf. The answers must demonstrate both nondiscriminatory intent and nondiscriminatory results—an uphill challenge, at best.

Should the EEOC find reasonable cause for the complaint, a conciliation agreement may be consummated: the employer may promise to cease from engaging in the questionable practice; the employer may agree to appropriate affirmative action to correct his discriminatory course; or the employer may agree to hire (or rehire) the aggrieved applicant (or employee), with or without back pay. Failure to reach agreement can result in the Commission's issuance of a "right to sue" letter, entitling the complainant to file a civil suit against the

employer within 90 days. Title VII is remedial and not puni-
tive, yet its muscle can devastate the violating employer.
Courts can award up to 2 years of back pay to huge groups
of female or minority employees. And affirmative action remedies may be awarded, setting precise and expensive time-
tables for hiring minorities and upgrading goals.

One very strong recommendation: initiate your own affirmative action program and a court will never need to do it for
you. Voluntary affirmative action programs are the best defense against any eventual equal employment opportunity
complaint, and they serve to make key personnel sensitive to
the law's requirements. What's more, by executive order, all
government contractors are required to undertake affirmative
action programs, reflecting special consideration for Vietnam
veterans and the handicapped.

9•5
TWO ACTS TO FOLLOW

The Equal Pay Act applies to employers of more than 25
persons and requires that pay be determined only on the basis
of skill (the experience, training, education, and ability required for the job), the effort actually expended on the job,
and responsibility.

The Age Discrimination Act allows discrimination on the
basis of age only when there is a "bona fide occupational qualification" (as there might be for an acting or modeling job)
and permits the imposition of physical fitness standards only
if they are not linked directly to age. Although benefits may
reasonably diminish with age, pursuant to a legitimate employee benefit plan (for instance, the same insurance dollars
can be used to buy a smaller policy for an older worker) an
employer may not reject an older job applicant merely because his employment might be more costly. And, without a
qualified retirement plan, involuntary retirement is prohibited until age 65.

Both acts are enforced by the U.S. Department of Labor. Its
Wage and Hour arm randomly surveys employers in interstate commerce and investigates complaints from all

sources. Much like the EEOC's procedure, the Labor Department negotiates settlements when it finds that violations have occurred. Employers who have made a settlement are well-advised to demand written releases from further action, or they may be subject to later litigation for back pay and other damages.

Remember to include the requirements of the Equal Pay Act and Age Discrimination Act in your voluntary affirmative action program.

9 • 6
WHAT IS OSHA?

Another broad employee-protective federal statute, the Occupational Safety and Health Act (OSHA), covers virtually all employers, except those whose health and safety standards are regulated by other laws. OSHA defines your general duty "to furnish a place of employment free from recognized hazards causing or likely to cause death or serious physical harm." A "recognized" hazard has judicially been interpreted as one that is preventable and generally known within an industry or to the public at large. While the hazard must be identifiable, it need not be obvious; airborne particles that can only be detected by delicate sensors are a "recognized" hazard.

Beyond this general duty, the Occupational Safety and Health Administration, a part of the Department of Labor, has promulgated specific industry standards. These are derived from data gathered by the Bureau of Statistics and from the continuing research conducted by the National Institute of Occupational Safety and Health. Contact the Government Printing Office directly for your free copies of "The OSHA General Industry Standards" and "The General Industry Guide for Applying Safety and Health Standards." The second title is published in six categories. You may choose: (1) workplace standards, (2) machines and equipment standards, (3) materials standards, (4) power source standards, (5) employee standards, and (6) process standards.

At the same time, request the "Fact Sheet for Small Businesses on Obtaining Compliance Loans" and, to help meet your reporting requirements, "What Every Employer Needs to Know About OSHA Recordkeeping."

Take advantage of the educational and training programs OSHA has spawned. The National Safety Council has developed courses in compliance procedure which are presented nationwide. Aided by private and public sponsors, some employers have been encouraged to set up their own programs in employee safety, in first aid, and in the assessment of working conditions. These voluntary steps are sensible—they are good morale boosters, they aid in OSHA compliance, and, in the long run, they maximize business productivity.

9•7
DOING BATTLE

In the years to come, OSHA will truly become a joint federal-state responsibility. As more and more states pass OSHA laws and build enforcement machinery, state agencies will assume a greater share of the inspection and adjudication functions. Right now, though, OSHA is largely a federal program.

Inspectors from the Occupational Safety and Health Administration randomly spot-check employer compliance—although the right to spot-check without warning is now being challenged—and investigate employee complaints. An employer is notified in writing of each specific violation and the time period fixed for its correction (the *abatement period*). Such *citation notices* must be posted by the employer for all employees to see. And a *notice of proposed penalty* may accompany the citation; the amount of the penalty will be determined by the size of the business, the gravity of the violation, the good faith of the employer, and the employer's history of previous violations. If the violation is not corrected within the abatement period, a *noncompliance notice* is issued and a substantial, additional penalty may be assessed on a daily basis.

A citation or penalty can be contested by notifying the Administration in writing of your intention to contest within 15 days after receiving a notice of proposed penalty. Then, you and your lawyer can contest any or all these elements:

1   *The citation.* You might contend that your mode of opera-
    tion is just as safe as the standard and request a perma-
    nent variance.
2   *The abatement period.* You can request an extension of
    time—or a temporary variance—by showing good reason
    for not complying within the allotted time.
3   *The proposed penalty.* You can challenge the amount of the
    penalty in light of the small size of your business, the
    relative insignificance of the violation, your good inten-
    tions, and your clean record.

After you notify the Administration of your intent to contest,
the matter will be docketed for a hearing before the OSHA
Review Commission, an independent federal agency, with
court-like trial procedures in force. Barring a last-minute
agreement with the Administration, you will be granted your
day in court.

9•8
A MORE PERFECT UNION

Even though management and labor depend on one another
for their very survival, they are normally in a state of conflict.
You and your co-owners (along with the high-level executives
you recruit) are dedicated to effecting cost economies wherever you can, and, as owners of capital, you may claim both
the right and the obligation to decide how best to use that
capital. Your rank-and-file employees, on the other hand, will
strive for the best compensation package and working conditions they can, and, since their jobs may be lost to business
reverses, they may feel they are entitled to have some influence on decisions. Generally speaking, no one employee can
usurp managerial authority. But a united organization of employees can effectively bargain with employers to gain a major
role in business decision making.

Employers have traditionally resisted attempts to unionize
as threats to their right to manage and as assaults on their
pocketbooks. Your reaction to the preliminary steps taken by

your employees will make all the difference in your long-term employee relations and in the ongoing productivity and profitability of your business.

9 • 9
YOUR UNION STRATEGY

Before a union representative pays you a visit, he will probably have gathered the signatures of at least 30 percent of the employees in the proposed "bargaining unit." They will have given authorization for the union to petition the National Labor Relations Board for an election by secret ballot if you refuse to recognize the union. (A 30 percent response is a sufficient show of interest to support a petition; a 50 percent response might allow union recognition, even without an election.)

With authorizations in hand, the representative will inform you of his success. Keep the encounter brief and civil. Listen to any demands and let the representatives know that you must discuss them with your lawyer before making a commitment.

If you and your lawyer have any reasonable doubt that the union is the collective-bargaining choice of a majority of the workers in a legally cognizable bargaining unit, he will draft a refusal to recognize the union. Although your refusal to recognize a union that legitimately represents a majority can lead to later charges of unfair labor practices, recognizing a union that does *not* represent the majority is also illegal. When in doubt, opt for the refusal and let the NLRB conduct a secret election to determine the union's true status.

Once the union representative files his petition, you will receive an NLRB questionnaire seeking to learn whether your operation meets the Board's self-imposed jurisdictional standards. If it does, you may request a hearing to test whether or not the voting unit (those workers who will be eligible to vote) is a true bargaining unit over which the Board should maintain jurisdiction. Finally, if all is in order, an election agreement will be signed, explicitly defining the bargaining unit and setting the election date.

9 • 10
ON THE CAMPAIGN TRAIL

During the 30 days or so between the election agreement's execution and the balloting, you will probably conduct a "soft-sell" anti-union campaign. It should be both thoughtful and deliberate. You will be careful to avoid any unfair tactics: improper conduct can induce the NLRB to set aside a management victory; and your repeated violations of the National Labor Relations Act can force union recognition, even without an election. So, conduct an issues-oriented campaign under your lawyer's guidance, and concentrate on these points:

- ✓ Play up all the benefits your employees enjoy; they may not understand them fully.
- ✓ Cite the advantage of dealing with you on a personal, one-to-one basis, rather than with a large, impersonal union, with its own rules and regulations.
- ✓ Compare your employees' wages and benefits with your competitors' programs. If you have been more generous, drive that fact home; if you haven't been, explain why. No union can win more for its members than an employer can afford to pay.
- ✓ Review the costs and other disadvantages of unionization. Your employees should be told about "one-man rule" (union bossism) if it applies, or seniority systems that penalize younger, ambitious workers.
- ✓ Point out that the ballot is secret, and that signing an authorization does not bind an employee to vote for union representation. But hasten to add that the majority will decide and their decision will not be held against any employee.
- ✓ Describe how difficult it is to remove a union if it is later decided not to be worth the effort and expense.
- ✓ Let your employees know that they are not obligated to speak with the union representative, and urge them to report any threats or coercion.
- ✓ Correct any rumors, misrepresentations, or distortions of fact with clear rebuttals. First quote the union's allegation

verbatim and then tell the truth. Your credibility should zoom.

9•11
TELLING YOUR STORY
But how do you get the word out? In each case, your message should be simple, straightforward, and personal, and should be carefully reviewed by your lawyer. These methods of communication are most successful:

⇒ *Letters.* Personal letters sent to employees' homes are always very effective. A final letter rebutting the union's principal charges can be mailed just before the election.

⇒ *Notes in pay envelopes.* This is a good way to relate union costs to take-home pay.

⇒ *Handbills.* If distribution by the union is prohibited in certain work areas, voluntarily impose the same restriction on yourself.

⇒ *Movies.* Some popular anti-union movies have been held "inflammatory" and thus unfair, so get your lawyer's OK before showing any movie.

⇒ *Speeches.* Speeches are perhaps the most effective way, but they must not be coercive, nor may they be delivered within 24 hours of the election.

9•12
KEEPING IT CLEAN
Union elections are to be free and open. Unfair campaign tactics are prohibited. Here are a few examples of behavior recently held to be unfair:

x You may not poll employees about their sympathies, but do listen to any unsolicited information your employees voluntarily offer.

x You may not threaten or imply a loss of jobs or benefits (or, for that matter, predict the company's failure) after a union victory. Nor may you promise extraordinary wage increases or other benefits after a union defeat.

x   In the broadest sense, don't spy. No management person-
    nel should ever attend a union meeting, and no employer
    representative can be present in the voting area during
    the election.

x   Once an election agreement has been signed, you may not
    withhold employees' names and addresses from the union
    organizers.

x   You may not visit employees at their homes to talk against
    the union.

x   While you may establish reasonable rules about solicita-
    tion and the distribution of materials in work areas and on
    company time, they must be applied fairly and uni-
    formly to union and management alike. And any re-
    striction must be clearly posted for all to see.

x   You may neither favor anti-union employees nor dis-
    criminate against pro-union employees. To avoid dis-
    crimination charges, your lawyer may advise you to fire no
    one during the campaign.

x   While you will not be dispassionate, you may not issue
    statements that are untrue, misrepresentative or, foggiest
    of all, "inflammatory."

9 • 13
THE ELECTION AND ITS AFTERMATH

The NLRB will do its best to ensure that both the campaign
and the election are carried out democratically and by its
rules. The election will be conducted by a Board agent, with
one observer present from each side. Yet the outcome may not
be the final word.

If you are successful, the union may attempt a reversal in
one of three ways:

1   It is illegal to refuse to recognize a union unless you
    genuinely believe it does not represent the majority. The
    union may contend it had sufficient authorizations before
    the election, and that your "refusal to bargain" at that
    time should force recognition now.

2   The union may charge you with unfair labor practices,
    entitling it to a new election.

3   Or, the union may retreat and regroup.

If the union is successful, you too have your options:

1   You may file an unfair labor practices charge against the union and attempt to have the election set aside. Of course, the charges must be substantial and supported by evidence.

2   You may sell your business and subject the purchaser to the burdens of a union shop, as well as any liability for pending charges of unfair labor practices.

3   You can go out of business, but closing down only part of it or moving out of state may be an illegal union-avoidance scheme.

4   Or, most realistically, you may recognize the union and commence good-faith collective bargaining.

9•14
THE DUTY TO BARGAIN

The Wagner Act requires an employer to "bargain collectively with the representatives of his employees" and that such bargaining is to be "in respect to rates of pay, wages, hours of employment, or other conditions of employment." An amendment to the Taft-Hartley Act defines collective bargaining as

> . . . the performance of the mutual obligation of the employer and the representative of the employees to meet at reasonable times and confer in good faith with respect to wages, hours, and other terms and conditions of employment, or the negotiation of an agreement, or any question arising thereunder, and the execution of a written contract incorporating any agreement reached if requested by either party, but such obligation does not compel either party to agree to a proposal or require the making of a concession. . . .

Bad faith, then, can be shown by "surface bargaining"—avoiding the real issues, delaying tactics, refusing to discuss "mandatory" issues (including wages, hours, fringes, union security and plant rules), refusing to make counterproposals, or declaring one's intent not to reach an agreement.

Any party found guilty of bad faith bargaining by the NLRB can expect the assessment of penalties and economic retaliation in the form of a work stoppage. Employees may legally strike, but may not conduct a wildcat strike or slow-down, nor may they strike in violation of an existing no-strike clause or an NLRB-declared 60-day cooling-off period. And employees who strike because of their employer's bad faith bargaining may have rights to reinstatement. An employer has the equivalent right to lockouts, a last-gasp weapon which is technically regulated and, like a strike, brings economic suffering to both sides. And, for better or worse, a threatened or existing work stoppage may bring the Federal Mediation and Conciliation Service into the bargaining arena as a go-between.

9•15
THE UNION CONTRACT

Whether negotiations come easily or not, the collective-bargaining agreement should be your assurance of a smooth relationship with your employees throughout its term. Your attorney will negotiate from strength and fairness and will arrive at an agreement both sides can live with. At least some of these issues will be resolved:

⇒ *Conditions of recognition.* There will be a clear definition of which employees constitute the bargaining unit.

⇒ *Union security.* Taft-Hartley requires that any *"check-off"* provision authorizing union dues deductions from employer paychecks be included in the agreement and OK'd by employees. A "check-off" can cover only a one-year period, and *hot cargo clauses*—by which unions can refuse to handle struck work—are illegal altogether.

⇒ *Union activities.* The ground rules for the conduct of union affairs will be fully set out.

⇒ *Working conditions.* This may be the meat and potatoes of the agreement. Job classifications, subcontracting provisions, plant rules, hiring and firing, seniority systems—all these and more will be fully explored.

⇒ *Wages.* This topic may be covered in the contract proper or in an appendix or separate agreement that can more easily be reviewed annually and amended. Either way, the sticky issue of overtime and holidays and their respective rates of pay will be tackled.

⇒ *Health and welfare benefits.* The agreement will include a detailed explanation of coverages and who is covered; Taft-Hartley will again control any payroll deductions. Company policy on sick leave, funeral leave, and jury duty will also be specified.

⇒ *Management clause.* The rights and responsibilities of management will be itemized, as will the decision areas outside union jurisdiction.

⇒ *Grievance procedure.* A grievance will be defined, along with the step-by-step procedure for its adjudication.

⇒ *Arbitration procedure.* Again, the process will be exhaustively detailed and will include pre-arbitration procedures, time limits for arbitration requests, the scope of arbitrators' authority, the arbitrator selection method, and more.

⇒ *No-strike and picket-line clauses.* Careful drafting can eliminate the loopholes that often plague these areas.

⇒ *Nondiscrimination clause.* The contract will comply with the equal employment opportunity laws. (See sections 9•2 and 9•3)

9•16
THE END RESULT

Again, there is a merger of objectives: business meets its social obligations and, at the same time, provides its employees with opportunity, security and status. Whether benefits and conditions are negotiated individually or collectively, the end result is a more fruitful employment relationship and, in the long run, a more successful business. So the law's requirements and the goals of the entrepreneur never need collide.

10

HANDLING
THE EXECUTIVE
TEAM

*Leadership is the ability to get men to do what they don't
want to do and like it.*

—Harry Truman

10•1
DOING IT RIGHT

Management is leadership. And your ability to attract and
develop top-notch people will have greater bearing on your
success in business than anything else.

Your unique organization and operation of the management team can set you apart from your peers. Start at the
beginning with a formal, contractual relationship with every
team player who's got it in him to help make you a success.
The substance of the contract will vary from business to business, but here are a few important topics you and your lawyer
should consider in drafting any executive employment
agreement:

⇒ *Duties and responsibilities.* Try to avoid duplication of effort,
and agree right from the start about how much authority
each executive is to have. But remember, the world turns,
so reserve the right to make changes.

140

⇒ *Best efforts.* Demand a full day's effort for a full day's pay.

⇒ *Noncompetition.* Insist on a restrictive covenant, prohibiting competition for a reasonable time after employment ends. The antitrust laws will strike down any clause held unreasonable in time or geography, so work with your lawyer in defining the minimum you need to be safe.

⇒ *Trade secrets.* These are your property, and so are your customer lists. Have your key people acknowledge your ownership and grant you the right to injunctive relief for any infringement. (See section 4 • 5)

⇒ *Term.* Choose a short, fixed term to start; you can always renew. And retain the right to end the relationship—for misconduct, nonperformance, disability, or other commonsense reasons.

⇒ *Compensation.* Set out in great detail the base salary, any automatic adjustments, payment frequency, bonuses, deferred comp, fringes, and forfeiture provisions. When stock is part of the package, the corporation should be given the "right of first refusal" of your employee's shares should he die, resign, retire, go bankrupt, or simply want to sell them. And he should be bound to join in the sale of stock in the event the corporation's controlling owners elect to sell out.

10 • 2
CASHING IN

Attracting good employees involves obvious, but never simple, techniques. Design a compensation package that will give high-level employees the financial security and self-esteem they need to do a good job for you, and you will have no trouble recruiting and training all the talent you need. The executives who help you run your show will become highly motivated and will contribute to increased productivity and increased profits for all of you to share.

But developing a compensation package is rarely a simple task. Cash on the barrelhead is the traditional way to pay employees. And, under today's federal tax laws, cash is an easy and attractive way to compensate executives. Our income tax rates reach as high as 70 percent. Yet usually no more than

a 50 percent tax rate—the "maximum tax" rate—applies to
the top dollar of "personal service income."

10 • 3
BONUSES NOW AND THEN

After a realistic base salary, many businesses pay their executives *current cash bonuses,* which are tied to company profits.
The employee is thus given a genuine incentive (one that is
subject to the "maxi-tax"), and the employer can deduct it all
in the year it is paid. One disadvantage: executives can claim
current bonuses that aren't contingent upon future service
and then move on to graze elsewhere.

One often proposed solution is the *deferred bonus,* paid over
a period of years starting after it is earned, usually after retirement. A deferred bonus can be made expressly subject to
forfeiture by an executive who leaves prematurely. At first
blush, deferral may appear especially desirable, since the employee may net more of his bonus dollars after retirement,
when he might be in a lower tax bracket. But abandon that
widely held belief. The fact is that a deferred bonus is taxable
to 50 percent, just the same as a current bonus is . . .
and, when the retired executive receives qualified retirement
plan benefits and income from outside investments along with
his bonus, 50 percent may become his tax rate anyway.

In weighing the relative merits of a deferred bonus plan,
look at these problems too:

x   The whole point of the plan—retaining your truly excep-
    tional executives—can be undercut by a hungry compet-
    itor who is willing to match your deferred payout.
x   Your top executives might resent your padlocking them.
x   They might question your ability to pay up when their
    time comes.
x   Employees will gripe about your eventual payment in dis-
    counted, inflated dollars. One answer: in the interim, in-
    vest the deferred funds for them.
x   A forfeiture clause can backfire, forcing a marginal em-
    ployee to stay when he might otherwise leave.

10•4
SHARING YOUR SHARES

Another way to foster longevity among corporate executives is through the use of *restricted stock*. Grant your key employees the right to buy shares of your company's stock at a bargain price. The catch is that, if they quit before a certain date, they must sell their shares back to the company for what they paid. Only at their target date would your employees pay a tax (subject to the 50 percent maxi-tax) on the difference between the value of their shares then and the amount they paid for them.

10•5
OPTING FOR OPTIONS

Stock options provide another means of compensation. The Tax Reform Act of 1976 repealed the *qualified stock option* rules for employee stock options granted after May 20, 1976. Now, the value of any new option is taxed as ordinary income to the employee when it is granted, as long as it has an ascertainable fair-market value. And the Senate-House conferees instructed the Treasury to "make every reasonable effort to determine a fair market value for an option." If it has no readily ascertainable fair-market value at that time, it won't be taxed until it's exercised by the employee. The tax will be based on the difference between the option price and the stock's fair-market value.

Look at these advantages:

✔ Although the employee receives taxable income at the time of the exercise, the employer earns a tax deduction, which often leads it to grant more shares than it otherwise could.

✔ The employee can enjoy an automatic profit at the time of the grant.

✔ The employee is taxed at lower capital gain rates on any appreciation after the exercise date.

Resist the conclusion that all your compensation choices are hopelessly muddled and ineffective. Clearly, conflicting tax and business objectives will force you into some fancy foot-work, and no option approach will be ideal. Creative lawyers are forever devising new ways of meeting those often inconsistent challenges. Here are a few worth investigating:

- *Seesaw options* cause each dollar increase in a share's market value to trigger a dollar drop in the option price.
- *Performance shares* earmark stock certificates for key executives, certificates that will become theirs at a future date if profit contingencies are met. With the shares, executives earn taxable income and their employer gains a like tax deduction.
- *Deferred stock bonuses* award shares now, to be delivered at a later date. At transfer time, the employee is taxed at ordinary rates and the employer deducts the amount of that income.
- *Phantom stock plans* grant to select employees hypothetical shares of stock and the dividends they would earn. At a later date, the dollar amount of appreciation in the market value of the phantom shares (and their phantom earnings) over their value when they were credited to employee accounts is paid out in cash. This is a deferred cash bonus, with appreciation in corporate stock measuring the amount of the payout. Phantom stock plans are favored by publicly held companies, which need not determine a "market value" by formula; closely held companies will usually opt for a deferred cash plan.

10 • 6
SOME PERKY PERKS

No longer do "dollars now" and "dollars then" constitute the enlightened employer's compensation program. Yesterday's fringes are today's indispensables. Yet every business is plagued by the competing demands of cash outflow, capital requirements, and earnings objectives. And every business must relate its net after-tax cost of employee salaries and perquisites to employees' net after-tax benefits. These perks—

tax-free to the employee, but deductible by the employer— are particularly cost-effective:

- *Medical/dental/hospitalization plans.* A basic group health in-surance plan is an indispensable fringe for all employees. Pursuant to a written plan, a corporation may also pay or reimburse any health costs of eligible corporate em-ployees and deduct its full out-of-pocket expense. This is one benefit that can be exclusively afforded officers, with-out constituting taxable income to them.
- *Life insurance coverage.* A corporation can deduct the pre-miums for up to $50,000 in group term insurance on the lives of at least ten employees in designated classes, and they will realize no taxable income. Beyond $50,000, the corporation may still take a tax deduction, but the em-ployee pays a tax on the excess value—still a tax-favored bargain.

  Whole-life insurance premiums are deductible by the employer if they are part of an employee's reasonable com-pensation, and the employee will be personally taxed on them. Split-dollar insurance can be purchased by an em-ployer who pays only the part of the premium that repre-sents the increase in cash value; the employee pays the balance. The proceeds become payable to the corporation (to the extent of its investment) and to the employee's beneficiary.
- *Wage-continuation plans.* In the case of incapacity, the em-ployee would receive tax free up to $5,200 sick pay each year, reduced dollar for dollar by adjusted gross income (including disability income) over $15,000. This reduc-tion, new under the Tax Reform Act of 1976, may well eliminate the benefit for most executives.
- *Moving expenses.* The expenses incurred in house-hunting, in renting temporary lodging, and in selling an old resi-dence and purchasing a new one are generally deductible by the employer and the employee. Any nondeductible excess can be structured as additional pay to the employee.

⤙ *Education.* The cost of in-house seminars is tax deductible
by the employer and tax free to the employee. Grants for
outside study are deductible too, but only if the program
improves the employee's skill without qualifying him for a
new occupation.

⤙ *Travel and entertainment.* Reasonable expenses in promoting the employer's business are deductible by it and tax
free to the employee. What matters here is your ability to
document the time, place, purpose, and participants.

⤙ *Automobiles.* An employer can depreciate a company car
and deduct all its running costs. The employee receives
taxable income only to the extent the car is put to incidental personal use. One note: when the driver is a
shareholder-employee, the corporation may not deduct
the personal-use portion of any car expense.

⤙ *Low-interest or interest-free loans.* Loans for home purchasing and outside investment are often a tax-free benefit
that any business unit can offer its key personnel. But
consult with counsel first; this practice is riddled with tax
pitfalls.

⤙ *Financial advice.* The employer may deduct the cost of
employee counseling, but the employee realizes report-
able taxable income equal to its value, which becomes an
itemized deduction on his personal tax return. Financial
counseling is gaining swift acceptance as a fringe, since it
increases spendable employee income and thus sweetens
the whole comp package.

⤙ *Prepaid legal expenses.* Employees can receive legal services
tax free pursuant to a qualified group legal-services plan.

10•7
WHEN YOU ARE THE EMPLOYEE

A nondeductible expense can effectively cost about twice as
much as a deductible one, so tax deductibility can maximize
the output of every dollar you budget for the upper
echelon—including yourself. The Internal Revenue Code allows an employer to deduct "expenses paid or incurred during the taxable year in carrying on any trade or business,

including a reasonable allowance for personal services actually rendered."

What is "reasonable" and when compensation is "for personal services actually rendered" are issues the IRS frequently raises in claiming that a corporate shareholder-employee's paycheck is really a disguised nondeductible dividend. To safeguard tax deductibility, take these steps:

⇒ At least annually, adopt a compensation package by a resolution of the directors (one of whom might well be independent). Define its elements and cite its underlying philosophy.

⇒ Record any special factors justifying big salaries—long hours of work, unique abilities, experience and qualifications, any other employee pluses. The IRS will consider these, along with industry comparisons and economic conditions, in judging "reasonableness."

⇒ Establish a clear dividend policy, and salaries will less likely be viewed as hiding a return on your business investment. Many small corporations pay a token dividend every year, just to help counter such a challenge.

⇒ The directors should authorize any bonuses, and employment contracts should support any contingent payments to employees, especially shareholder-employees.

⇒ Finally, the corporation should enter into *reimbursement agreements,* such as this one, with all shareholder-employees:

Compensation payments or reimbursements made to the officer that are disallowed, in whole or in part, as a deductible expense by the Internal Revenue Service, shall be reimbursed by him to the full extent of the disallowance. It shall be the duty of the Board of Directors to enforce the repayment of each such amount disallowed. A payment shall be deemed to be disallowed only when the time has lapsed for an appeal from or review of the adverse decision of the last tribunal or agency to consider the issue.

If compensation is deemed nondeductible by the corporation, it is returned and made available for redistribution at another time, and perhaps in another way.

10 • 8
RETIREMENT PLANNING: A DOZEN DEMANDS

The bedrock of any comp package is usually the company retirement program. The prominence of retirement planning as a high-level compensation tool derives from the "qualification" of certain formalized retirement programs. Qualified retirement plans are those that meet rigid IRS standards and the sweeping tax and labor principles of the Employee Retirement Income Security Act (ERISA). Corporate employer contributions to a qualified plan are currently deductible; the earnings of such contributions grow tax free; and benefiting employees defer personal taxation on their allocable shares of both contributions and earnings until later in life, when a favorable tax rate applies.

These are the basic requirements for a qualified retirement program:

1 The plan must be formal and in writing.
2 It must be communicated to employees.
3 The plan must be maintained for the exclusive benefit of employees and their beneficiaries.
4 The plan must be nondiscriminatory in coverage. Generally, 70 percent of all employees must be covered or 70 percent of all employees must be eligible and 80 percent of all eligible employees covered. An exception: union employees may be excluded if their retirement benefits were collectively bargained in good faith.
5 The plan must be nondiscriminatory in operation, too. This simply means that contributions, benefits, and forfeitures cannot be allocated in a way that irrationally favors shareholder-employees and managers.

The reason that qualified plans are nevertheless viewed as executive fringes is that all kinds of discrimination are permissible. For one thing, contributions and benefits can be tied to salary levels. For another, most plan's benefits can be integrated with Social Security benefits, altogether bypassing employees who earn less than the Social Security tax base. Integration is not prohibited, since everyone is treated alike—some through the public system, others through the private.

6 Ordinarily, employees must become eligible to participate after one year of service or upon reaching age 25, whichever comes later.

7 All employee contributions must "vest" (become irretrievably theirs) immediately. And employer contributions typically must (1) vest fully after 10 years, or (2) vest 25 percent after 5 years, 5 percent for each of the next 5 years, and 10 percent for the next 5, or (3) vest 50 percent when an employee's years of service and age total 45, and 10 percent each year thereafter. Fifty percent vesting after 10 years of service and 100 percent vesting after 15 years is always a must.

8 The plan must provide for a *joint and survivorship annuity* for at least half the amount payable to each participating employee. Under the annuity the employee receives payments for a designated period or for life. Upon his death, his beneficiary receives payments for the rest of the period or life.

9 The plan must not exceed statutory limits on contributions and benefits.

In *defined-contribution plans* (profit-sharing and stock-bonus plans) annual contributions for a participant cannot exceed $25,000 (or such greater amount as the Secretary of the Treasury OK's) or 25 percent of the year's total compensation. Annual contributions include forfeitures, employer contributions, and either (1) half the employee contributions or (2) employee contributions that exceed 6 percent of compensation, whichever is lower.

In *defined-benefit plans* (pension plans) annual benefits, funded in accordance with statute, may not exceed $75,000 or the average of the highest three years' compensation, whichever is lower.

10 Plan assets other than insurance contracts must be held in a trust managed by a bank, insurance company, or bonded fiduciary. The trustee is obliged to act for the

exclusive benefit of plan participants as a "prudent man" would, conservatively diversifying his portfolio. And, among other things, it is his duty to avoid suspect trust transactions with himself, with the employer and its officers, with directors and with 10-percent shareholders. These transactions might include any sale, exchange, or lease of property, the lending of money or any extension of credit, and the furnishing of goods, most services, and facilities.

11 Qualification carries with it all kinds of reporting obligations. After IRS approval, participants must receive a clear summary of the plan, including vesting standards. A complete description must be filed with the Department of Labor within 120 days, and any change must be reported within 60 days. An annual report must also be filed with the IRS, and actuarial reports for defined-benefit plans must be filed at least every three years. The Pension Benefit Guarantee Corporation, the insurer of vested benefits for all defined-benefit plans except professional service corporation plans, also requires annual reports, as well as notice of any impending curtailment or termination of benefits.

12 Should the plan be terminated, participants must be fully vested in their accrued benefits, and assets must be allocated according to ERISA guidelines.

10•9
VARIATIONS ON THE THEME

The requirements for a retirement program are sticky, and the variations are many. Let's look at a few of the most popular concepts and see what they have to offer you:

✔ *Profit-sharing plans.* Your corporation can contribute and deduct a slice of its profits—up to 15 percent of its payroll—to a trust. Decide exactly how much to contribute each year; you need not commit yourself to a specific formula as long as contributions are substantial and recurring. The trustee will credit each participant's individual account with his share of any employer contribution and its tax-exempt earnings. And the participant may supplement the corporate contribution with a voluntary employee contribution, which also earns him tax-free investment income. Upon an employee's death, retirement, or disability, all that's in his account will be paid out, in a tax-favored distribution.

✔ *Stock bonus plans.* Employer contributions need not be tied to profits, and distributions must be made in employer stock. Otherwise, qualified stock bonus plans work like profit-sharing plans.

✔ *Employee stock ownership plans* (ESOP's). Here, employees truly share in the ownership of corporate capital. The corporation contributes its stock and deducts its fair market value, up to 15 percent of its payroll. The eventual out-of-trust distributions to employees are likewise in employer stock. While an ESOP may mean the dilution of your shareholdings, it will allow your corporation to borrow money repayable in pretax dollars, and, at the same time, to increase cash flow, refinance debts, and supply a ready market for corporate stock. (See section 11•3)

✔ *Money-purchase pensions.* Make contributions by formula (normally a percentage of compensation) and deduct them. Unlike profit-sharing plans, participants in a money-purchase pension plan do not share forfeitures; instead, they serve to reduce future employer contributions. Each participant's pension will be whatever could be purchased as an annuity by the money on hand at his retirement.

✔ *Pensions.* Base your plan on actuarially computed, deductible contributions, and provide benefits based on compensation, years of service, or both. Actuarial gains will reduce future corporate payins. And tax-favored distributions will be paid out to retirees, the disabled, and beneficiaries of employees who die while in your company's service.

10 • 10
RETIREMENT PLANNING FOR THE SELF-EMPLOYED

So much for the corporation. What about the proprietor and the partner? They too are eligible for a tax-sheltered retirement program—the HR–10 or Keogh Plan. Here's how it works:

⇒   A self-employed person may contribute on his own behalf up to 15 percent of his earned income or $7,500, whichever is less. He must then contribute the same percentage of earned income for all his covered employees.

⇒   All full-time, nonseasonal employees with three years of service must be covered. That's why many proprietors and partners pay their working spouses and children reasonable salaries, cover them under Keogh, and up their effective benefits.

⇒   Keogh contributions fully vest immediately. Any employee has an irrevocable right to his share, even if he is fired or quits.

⇒   Funding can be through the use of a trust, custodial accounts, nontransferable annuity contracts, U.S. Retirement Bonds, or investment company face-amount certificates.

⇒   Accumulations are tax free until distribution, which may be any time between the ages of 59½ and 70½, or at death or disability. And payouts are tax favored.

10 • 11
MEET IRA

Is everyone covered? Unfortunately not. The Congress was well aware that millions of Americans did not participate in qualified retirement plans when, as part of ERISA, it allowed them to set up their own *individual retirement accounts* (IRAs). IRAs have filled a big security void for people whose employers offer no qualified plan; through a special IRA rollover feature, for employees whose employers have terminated their plans; and, ironically, for proprietors and partners who prefer to salt away retirement dollars without subsidizing the benefit for every 3-year vet in their shops. The mechanics are straightforward:

⇒ Each year, contribute the lesser of 15 percent of your earned income or $1,500 to a trust or custodial account, or for annuity contracts or U.S. Retirement Bonds. Or, you may contribute up to $1,750 to an IRA that has a subaccount for the benefit of your spouse who doesn't work outside the home. Another alternative is to contribute up to $875 for your own IRA account and up to $875 to a separate account for your spouse who doesn't work outside the home.

⇒ Deduct your contribution from your gross income "above the line" and not as an itemized deduction.

⇒ Your contributions will grow tax free until distribution.

⇒ Your account balance will be distributed to you between ages 59½ and 70½ (or upon death or disability). While no kinder-than-usual tax rate will apply, you will be eligible for *income averaging*—a computation marvel that eases the tax bite in peak-income years.

10•12
A CLOSING COMMENT

The keys, then, are fairness and humanity. Take, but give too. Inspire your team to put out all that it can. Offer a reasonable, cost-effective, and motivating income package, and respond to the economic hazards of death, retirement, illness, and disability. Not only will you enhance your top employees' satisfaction with their work, but you will meet your social responsibilities in a way the outside world will commend. The employer, the employee, and the community will all become the beneficiaries of a profitable business strategy.

11

LOOKING AHEAD

Even if you're on the right track, you'll get run over if you just sit there.

—Will Rogers

11•1
DEBT vs. EQUITY

The successful are never content to stagnate, and so it is that the successful company will eventually begin to look for large infusions of new capital to increase its productivity. Yet the attraction of capital can be costly and even risky. Consider, for example, the relative merits of these financing techniques:

⇒ *Debt.* Debt financing is especially appealing to the prosperous corporation. Its cost—interest—is tax deductible and, although debt holders can impose controls, no dilution of ownership is suffered. For the investor, debt is the safest of all securities and offers tax-free recovery of investment, along with a "guaranteed," fixed rate of return.

Debt has many faces: short-term bank loans, leases and sale-leasebacks, mortgages, long-term private placements, debentures secured by the company's general credit, and bonds secured by specific assets. Each has its own rewards and drawbacks for both the business and the investor.

⇒   *Equity.* Equity financing means the sale of an ownership
interest and, with it, a reduction in control. It also means
the payment of dividends in expensive after-tax dollars.

On the other hand, equity financing can bring in tax-
free capital without imposing a fixed obligation on the
company, and that looks truly impressive on the financial
statement. Equity financing comes in various forms with
differing consequences:

Common stock offers the investor great volatility along
with great potential for capital appreciation. The holder of
common stock—last in line at liquidation—has the right
to vote along with you and can see his risk mitigated only
through the use of Section 1244 stock (section 2 • 7) or
Subchapter S stock (sections 2 • 8 and 2 • 9). Theoretically
at least, *preferred stock* is more conservative: the holder of
preferred stock has a claim to dividends and to the assets
upon liquidation that is superior to the claim of the
holder of common stock. Preferred shares vary as far as
rights are concerned: they may be voting shares; they
may be *cumulative,* requiring the company to make up
any dividends in arrears; they may be *callable,* redeem-
able by the company at a set price; or they may be *participating,* entitling the holder to share in any dividends
beyond a specified floor.

⇒   *Combos.* Imaginative lawyers have combined the advantages of debt and equity financing, and these combinations may provide the easiest way to attract investors.
Debentures or preferred stock, for instance, may be con-
vertible into common stock; the investor assumes a
smaller front-end risk, but may later share in capital
gain. The company, however, must tackle the tricky task
of setting a conversion price low enough to attract investors and high enough to circumvent a gross dilution.

Rights, options, and warrants serve the same purpose—
to offer the investor a relatively low-risk opportunity that
just might appreciate in the years to come. Finally, pack-
ages of debt and equity can help the investor hedge his
bet.

11•2
SEVEN GOOD CREDITORS

The issuance of debt is often thought to be the most desirable trade-off for investment capital, for, along with its other
virtues, it presupposes your continuing and exclusive
ownership of your business. Luckily, all kinds of pure-debt
opportunities may be yours for the asking:

⇨ Commercial banks offer letters of credit and short- and
   intermediate-term loans. (See section 7 • 13)
⇨ The federal government offers SBA loans, EDA loans,
   and many others. The Economic Development Administration (EDA), an agency of the Department of Commerce, provides business-development loans to assist
   economically deprived areas.
⇨ State and local governments offer development loans.
⇨ Equipment manufacturers and leasing companies offer
   leases and sale-leasebacks, which are desirable off-
   balance-sheet financing.
⇨ Factors finance receivables.
⇨ Trade suppliers may offer both credit and side loans.
⇨ And even tax-exempt organizations may offer grants and
   loans to certain select industries.

11•3
SHARING THE WEALTH

Once these sources have been exhausted, your options for
pure debt narrow, and those who want to share in your
equity become logical candidates. These are a few to consider:

⇨ *Insiders.* No doubt you will have already tapped your own
   bank account. Don't overlook those who work for you.
   Stock options (section 10 • 5) and ESOP's (section 10 • 9),
   to name two vehicles, can serve to reinvest employee-
   compensation expense in your future growth.
       An ESOP is a derivative of the qualified stock bonus
   plan, employing leveraging. Simply stated, the employer
   company (or majority shareholders) sells stock to an
   ESOP trust for cash; the trust borrows the purchase

price from a bank, using the stock as collateral; and the employer contributes an amount to the trust each year sufficient to repay the loan and interest. The annual contributions to the trust are effectively tax-deductible payments of principal and interest. And future appreciation in the value of the stock held by the trust is shared by plan participants.

ESOPs can leverage the purchase of another company, refinance existing debt, create a market for corporate stock, transfer control to key personnel upon the founder's retirement, purchase life insurance with pre-tax dollars, and take advantage of an 11 percent (rather than the usual 10 percent discussed in section 7•9) investment tax credit (if participants' interests vest fully and immediately, and if participants may vote their own shares).

At this writing, the fabulous Howard Hughes estate may form an ESOP and sell Hughes' Summa Corp. stock to its managers. The proceeds would be split among the IRS (to satisfy a $700 million estate tax bill) and the Hughes heirs. The result: the Hughes empire would remain intact and private.

⇒ *Private venture-capital firms.* These use their own resources to invest in relatively closely held enterprises that offer long-term big returns. Most prominent are Bessemer Securities Corporation, William A. Burden and Company, Charles River Partners, Davis and Rock, Greylock and Company, Parpon and Task, Rockefeller Brothers, and J. H. Whitney and Company.

⇒ *Venture-capital subsidiaries.* Large, diversified corporations provide capital to companies they intend to acquire at a later date.

⇒ *SBICs.* These have access to SBA money and get preferential tax treatment. They can take big risks to realize high interest on their debt position as well as the right to purchase equity. A word of warning: SBICs expect the right to major equity participation through conversion or separate warrants, and they impose strict controls. (See section 7•12)

⇒ *Pension funds.* Pensions are drowning in money, but cannot speculate.
⇒ *Insurance companies.* Ditto.
⇒ *The public.* As we will see, this can be the biggest and best source of all.
⇒ *Your competition.*

11•4
WHY MERGE?

Sharing your equity with others may be a fair exchange when they share their equity with you. And, more often than you might expect, unrelenting profits trigger the need to accelerate one's growth by acquiring or merging with a competitor, or even by being acquired by a competitor. Expansion spurs expansion. Motives vary, but these are the most frequently cited in buy-ins and sellouts.

⇒ *Diversification.* A merger or acquisition can enhance overall profitability and creditworthiness. What's more, the introduction of new products and services can help level peaks and valleys in profits and cash flow.
⇒ *Operating economies.* The combination of similar businesses can effect genuine cost economies and may increase the relative output of each employee.
⇒ *Access to assets.* It is often cheaper and always easier to buy, rather than to develop, a new product, contract rights, intellectual property, a competent sales force, and many other tough-to-build assets.
⇒ *Efficiencies.* A company's physical plant and systems will pay for themselves much faster once they are fully used, through the addition of new business.
⇒ *Tax advantages.* Under very strict rules, a buyer can acquire a seller's net operating loss carry-forward and use it to offset taxable income.
⇒ *Internal strife.* A sale or merger may be contemplated by a solid enterprise that is plagued by interowner dissension, or by a less-than-solid enterprise seeking a way out.
⇒ *Personal planning.* Retirement or estate planning objectives may require the diversification of one's personal

holdings or the creation of a liquid market for them. A sale or merger can do both.

11•5
A MORE PERFECT UNION

Tax law considerations, corporate law considerations, and antitrust law considerations coalesce in the structuring of a merger or acquisition. And so it is one of the most complex of legal transactions. In the broadest terms, there are three approaches worth examining.

An *asset acquisition* calls for the buyer's purchase of all or part of the seller's assets and business for cash, property, or securities. The seller's stock ownership and corporate structure remain intact until the seller is liquidated and the net sales proceeds are distributed to its shareholders.

THE PROS	THE CONS
Minority interests may be bypassed. Minority shareholders will usually have no veto, but merely the right to be bought out, and rarely will they have a right of appraisal.	An asset acquisition can be expensive: title to each asset must be separately transferred.
	Third-party consents are often required to transfer contracts, leases, and licenses.
Typically, the buyer's shareholders will not need to approve an asset acquisition.	Any of the seller's long-term debt that restricts a sale of assets may need to be recast.
The buyer will not assume the seller's undisclosed liabilities, or any liabilities it does not agree to assume.	Compliance under bulk-sales laws—protecting creditors against a debtor's selling of its business and absconding with the proceeds—will be required.
A purchase price allocation can offer substantial tax savings.	
	If buyer's securities serve as consideration, the transaction may later be viewed as a merger, voidable without proper notice to stockholders.

In a *stock acquisition,* the seller's shareholders sell all or part of their stock for cash, property, or the buyers' securities. Since the selling corporation is not a party to the transaction— its shareholders are—the seller's management need not approve. When they don't, it's called a takeover bid.

THE PROS

The transaction can be simple quick, and clean. The only documents that must be delivered are properly endorsed stock certificates.

No third-party approval need be obtained, since the corporation remains as before. Only the shareholders are new.

No directors' approval is required by the selling corporation.

The buyer does not directly assume corporate liabilities.

Installment income reporting may be available to sellers seeking to defer taxation if, in the year of the sale, payments to the sellers do not reach 30 percent of the price.

THE CONS

The sellers' corporation retains its liabilities.
Minority shareholders can hold out and retain a position in the sellers' corporation.

The purchase price cannot be allocated to specific assets to create a tax advantage for the buyer or sellers. And the buyer may be taxed on any depreciation recapture or investment-credit recapture on the sellers' assets.

SEC registration may be required if the selling corporation has more than a few shareholders.

A *statutory merger* is the combination of two corporations under a state's corporation laws. After both boards of directors and at least two-thirds of the shareholders of each corporation approve the merger, one survives, succeeding by operation of law to the assets and liabilities of the other. The disappearing corporation's stockholders exchange their shares for an equity position in the survivor. A *statutory consolidation* differs only in that both consolidating corporations disappear in favor of a new entity, which issues its stock in exchange for the shares of its predecessors.

THE PROS	THE CONS
Title to assets transfers automatically upon compliance with state formalities.	The survivor in a merger—or the consolidated new entity—assumes the obligations of any disappearing corporation.
Dissenting minority shareholders can be bought out for cash, and the buyer can be assured of acquiring full ownership.	The process can be slow and expensive: shareholders' meetings, sometimes with proxy materials and notices, must be conducted.
A wide range of securities may be issued without jeopardizing tax-free treatment.	Two-thirds approval of shareholders is generally required by statute and stubborn dissenters may promote a big cash drain.
Since either entity can survive a merger, nontransferable assets can easily be preserved.	The transaction must conform to state law, which may be limiting.
Required shareholders' meetings provide an opportunity to amend the charter and by-laws for the special purposes of the ongoing enterprise.	

11•6
THE TAX ANGLES

However the transaction is to be structured, price must be its cornerstone. Whether price is determined on the basis of book value, an independent appraisal, comparable price/earnings ratios within the seller's industry, or otherwise, the method of payment will, of course, significantly affect the net dollar result for both buyer and seller. A taxable acquisition, for example, gives the buyer a new basis in the stock or assets purchased, and the seller must recognize its own gain or loss. A "tax-free" acquisition transfers the seller's basis in its stock or assets to the buyer, and postpones taxation of the seller's gain or loss until the seller disposes of the securities received in payment.

Tax-free reorganizations include: *A-type consolidation or merger,* which complies with state law and meets Internal Revenue Code standards; *B-type stock acquisition,* in which the seller corporation exchanges at least 80 percent of its voting stock (and no other security) for voting stock of the buyer corporation (and no other security, property, or cash); and *C-type asset acquisition,* in which the buyer corporation acquires substantially all the assets of the seller corporation in exchange for the buyer's voting stock (and possibly a limited amount of other consideration).

Reorganization rules are tricky, but these basics must always be demonstrated:

1   There must be a continuity of interest, so the sellers must be paid in the stock of the buying corporation, and they must hold it.
2   There must be a continuity of business enterprise, meaning only that the acquired business must continue to operate.
3   There must be a non-tax business purpose, so tax avoidance may not be a central reason for the reorganization.

11•7
THE ISSUES WORTH NEGOTIATING

Taxable or tax free, a merger or acquisition invariably raises such diverse issues that setting a price and agreeing to a general structure are only the first skirmish in an intense bargaining campaign. You will spot these issues—and their resolution—in the acquisition contract your lawyer prepares for signature:

⇒   *The seller's representations.* The seller will warrant the legal status of its stock and the condition of its business as described in appended financial statements. In a stock-for-stock transaction, the shareholders will, of course, warrant their title to the shares they are selling.

Other warranties might include the ownership of the seller's assets and the physical condition of tangibles, the status of lawsuits and actions by government agencies, including the Internal Revenue Service, and, in a stock-for-stock transaction, the seller's investment purpose in acquiring the buyer's shares.

An investment-purpose warranty will help avoid the registration requirement under the Securities Act of 1933, and it will assure continuity of equity ownership for "pooling of interests" purposes. In a pooling of interests, the buyer's and seller's assets, liabilities and surpluses or deficits are aggregated. No new goodwill item is entered on the buyer's books, where the price exceeds the book value of the seller's assets, and no write-off is made against the buyer's after-tax earnings. The buyer can stay profit pretty.

⇒ *The buyer's representations.* Where the buyer is paying the seller in stock, the buyer will warrant that its stock is authorized and issued, fully paid and nonassessable.

⇒ *The assets.* The description of stock will be simple, but other assets may be difficult to define, and the purchase of assets demands an allocation of the purchase price to fix tax consequences (Exhibit A).

⇒ *The purchase price.* The price may be a predetermined dollar amount or number of shares. Or a formula may be adopted, setting the price as a function of the seller's future earnings or some other variable.

⇒ *An assumption of liabilities.* A stock purchase necessitates the assumption of all corporate liabilities: after all, there will be no change in the corporation's identity. A sale of assets, on the other hand, may or may not be accompanied by the buyer's assumption of certain of the seller's liabilities.

⇒ *The seller's indemnification.* The seller will typically indemnify the buyer against any unassumed liabilities in an assets purchase, and the seller's indemnification may be secured by a pledge of stock.

⇒ *Antitrust provisions.* Any past violation of the antitrust laws by the seller presents an assumption-of-liability question. And the antitrust laws are so sweeping that the seller's consistent compliance should be of real concern to the buyer: the Sherman Act prohibits combinations in restraint of trade—through price-fixing, territorial divisions, boycotts, and the like—and monopolies of commerce; the Federal Trade Commission Act prohibits unfair methods of competition and unfair or deceptive acts in commerce; and the Robinson-Patman Act prohibits price discrimination injurious to competition.

The acquisition itself may be in violation of the Clayton Act, which prohibits any corporation from acquiring another when the effect of the acquisition may be to lessen competition substantially or to tend to create a monopoly. The language of the Clayton Act has been broadly construed to apply not only to "vertical" combinations of competitors, but also to "horizontal" combinations of companies with a buyer-seller relationship (such as a wholesaler and a retailer); and to conglomerates—combinations of companies that sell noncompetitive but related products, or companies that sell similar products to different markets. The Act is violated whenever a merger or acquisition substantially lessens competition within a "line of commerce" (which may mean any product aimed at a target market) in any "section of the country," even a state or two. And a substantial lessening of competition is deemed to have occurred whenever a merger or acquisition notably increases an economic concentration, eliminates a substantial source of supply, eliminates a substantial factor in competition, or produces relationships between buyers and sellers that deprive competitors of a fair chance to compete.

The enforcement of federal antitrust laws is carried out by the Federal Trade Commission, the Justice Department, and through litigation in the private sector. And the FTC requires 60 days' written notice of any acquisition where the buyer's assets after the purchase would exceed $250 million.

Most advisers will recommend against seeking antitrust clearance from the Justice Department. Instead, when the buyer and seller fear that federal or competitor action may be instituted to enjoin their transaction, each may contractually retain the right to bow out gracefully upon information and belief that suit has been filed.

⇒ *Securities provisions.* The buyer in any acquisition calling for securities as payment is an "issuer" of securities, and is obligated to register them with the Securities and Exchange Commission, unless it qualifies for a specific exemption. The kind of registration or the specific exemption the issuer elects will affect the seller's ability to dispose of the securities it receives: only a full registration will allow the seller to liquidate its holdings without a hitch. Because of this increased liquidity, the seller will favor registration; because of the expenses and disclosure requirements registration would impose, the buyer will normally resist it. Should the seller prevail, the acquisition agreement will obligate the buyer to register its stock; should the buyer prevail, the agreement will provide that the buyer's stock certificates shall bear the legend:

> The shares represented by this certificate have not been registered under the Securities Act of 1933, as amended. The shares have been acquired for investment and may not be sold, offered for sale, or transferred in the absence of an effective registration statement for the shares under the Securities Act of 1933, as amended, or an opinion of counsel to the company that registration is not required under said Act.

If either party is subject to the Securities Act of 1934, detailed proxy material must be furnished to its shareholders and the SEC before the acquisition is voted upon. In any event, the Act's fraud provisions will probably apply, including the notorious Rule 10b, which states that, in connection with the purchase of any security:

> It shall be unlawful for any person, directly or indirectly, by the use of any means or instrumentality of interstate commerce, or of the mails, or of any facility of any national securities exchange:
>
> 1. To employ any device, scheme, or artifice to defraud,
>
> 2. To make any untrue statement of a material fact or omit to state a material fact necessary in order to

make the statement made, in the light of the circumstances under which they were made, not misleading
or,

3. To engage in any act, practice, or course of business
   which operates or would operate as a fraud or deceit
   upon any person.

Simply stated, the rule prohibits anyone in the buyer's
or seller's camp from taking advantage of inside information or failing to disclose material information.

Federal securities laws, state "blue sky" laws, and stock
exchange disclosure and shareholder-approval rules demand conservative compliance. Where registration is to be
avoided, a cautious seller may seek a "no action" letter
from the SEC. Application may be made to Chief Counsel,
Division of Corporate Finance, Securities and Exchange
Commission, Washington, D.C. 20025.

⇒ *Employee provisions.* The acquisition agreement should ensure the retention of key personnel through the assignment and delivery of employment contracts.

Any collective-bargaining agreement signed by the
seller should be reviewed carefully by the buyer's attorney.
It may be binding upon the buyer as a successor employer, even if not specifically assumed.

The seller's retirement plans should be transferred to
the buyer and, ideally, integrated into the buyer's existing
program. The liability for any of the seller's outstanding
stock options may be assumed by the buyer, which would
substitute its own options. Or it may assume no liability
for outstanding options.

⇒ *Noncompetitive agreement.* The buyer will seek the seller's
assurance that it will not compete in the business the
seller is acquiring. The buyer should propose language
that will not violate restraint-of-trade principles, for fear
of unenforceability and antitrust repercussions. The
seller, of course, will want any covenant to be narrowly
drafted so as to permit its normal growth without undue
impediment.

⇒ *Conduct pending the close.* The seller will be called upon to operate its business only in its ordinary course until title is transferred, and will be precluded from otherwise selling any of its assets. Farsighted counsel will allow exceptions for any beneficial capital expenditures known to be in the offing when the agreement is signed.

⇒ *Conditions precedent.* Both sides may require certain acts or events to take place before they are legally bound to follow through with the transaction. The buyer, for instance, may first insist on a pooling-of-interests opinion from the SEC and, of course, an accountant's certification.

The seller may require an opinion from the buyer's attorney confirming the buyer's corporate structure and validating the buyer's warranties. Or the seller may request a tax-free reorganization ruling from the Internal Revenue Service.

⇒ *Brokerage.* If a broker participated in the transaction, the party responsible for his fee should indemnify the other from any claim.

⇒ *Nuts and bolts.* Many other requirements may come to the fore:

— There should be compliance with bulk sales laws, or, at least, the seller should indemnify the buyer from any adverse consequences of noncompliance. (See section 1 • 9)

— The parties should agree on who is liable for any sales and use taxes assessed on account of the acquisition.

— Agreement should be reached about responsibility for the completion of pending customer contracts.

And on and on.

11•8
PRIVATE PLACEMENTS

When a merger or acquisition cannot fill the bill, or when a business combination creates a need for ready cash, the time may be right for a public or private offering. A *private placement* is any offering or sale of a security (any investment instrument) that is exempt from the expensive registration requirements of the Securities Act of 1933 as a "transaction by an issuer not involving any public offering." Usually a less disruptive move than a merger, a private placement can be a cheaper and faster way to gain outside financing than a conventional public offering, and its timing need not depend on the availability of audited financial statements and the workload of the SEC staff. What's more, a privately held company need make no public disclosure of its private offering.

Nearly all businesses issue securities, and almost all securities are exempt from registration. So private placements account for the vast majority of the securities issued in this country today. Yet, ironically, few areas of the law have been more treacherous for lawyers and their business clients. Let this be your primer:

First: Section 5 of the Securities Act of 1933 requires that any security be registered with the SEC before it is offered, sold, or delivered by use of the mails or facilities of interstate commerce, unless an exemption is available.

Second: Section 4(2) creates an exemption for private placements between an issuer and a few (usually no more than 25) sophisticated purchasers who are acquiring securities for investment and not for resale. Investment intent should be documented by restrictive legends on stock certificates, written instructions to the transfer agent, and investment letters from investors.

Third: Rule 146 sets out a more objective set of criteria:

1   No more than 35 persons (other than $150,000 purchasers and certain related persons) may buy securities in a given offering.
2   All offerees (and not just purchasers) must be able to evaluate the investment's merits and risks and bear those risks, including the risks of illiquidity and complete loss.
3   All offers must follow a specific form.
4   Offerees must be permitted access to the information any registration statement would provide.
5   The issuer must do its best to prevent a later public distribution.

Fourth: Rule 240 exempts small, limited transactions from registration. The aggregate sales price of all the issuer's securities in the past year cannot exceed $100,000, and all the issuer's securities, both before and after the transaction, must be beneficially owned by 100 or fewer persons. Again, the securities, which must be restricted as to reoffer and resale, may not be offered or sold by means of "general advertising," and no commission may be paid in connection with the sale. Each calendar year, an issue relying on Rule 240 must file an informational notice with the Commission's regional office.

Fifth: Exemption under the 1933 Act means exemption from its registration requirements. Compliance with its all-encompassing antifraud pronouncements will warrant the preparation of a numbered offering letter, circular, or prospectus that makes full disclosure of the transaction.

11•9
THE PUBLIC CHALLENGE

Suppose, for whatever reason, you can't take advantage of the private placement exemption or the *intrastate* exemption, which is the hard-to-come-by way out where a security is part of an issue offered and sold only to persons resident within a single state by an issuer who is a resident of or that is incorporated and doing business within the same state. Suppose also that other "safe harbors" under the federal securities laws don't apply to you. Are you prepared to undertake a full-blown public offering? It may be awfully tempting:

- Going public yields money galore—for R&D, for the retirement of existing debt, for expansion, for diversification.
- Future financing becomes so much easier. An initial offering will typically improve corporate net worth and borrowing power. And the creation of a public market with decent performance in the continuing after-market will facilitate the raising of additional equity capital.
- A publicly held company can acquire other companies for its own securities, without depleting its cash.

✔ The attraction and retention of key personnel can be aided by offering stock and stock-option opportunities in a publicly held company.

✔ The public ownership of your company will enhance its prestige, and your important customers and suppliers may become shareholders, more convinced than ever about your future growth.

✔ Your once illiquid investment in your business will be highly liquid, and perhaps more valuable than you ever dreamed.

On the other hand:

x Going public is expensive, and being a publicly held company is expensive. The legal and accounting fees for proxy materials, annual reports to shareholders, and the necessary SEC filings are costly and time-consuming. There are also fees of the transfer agent, registrar, and public relations consultant, as well as the cost of your time devoted to shareholder relations.

x Going public will require prior and ongoing disclosure of your salary, corporate transactions with management, and any potential conflicts of interest. Rarely, however, will the disclosure of profits, operating procedures, and important contracts place a company at a competitive disadvantage, as management sometimes fears.

x There is a real possibility of loss of control. Voting trusts and multiple classes of stock may mitigate the effects of dilution, but, in the long run, management control may nonetheless be eroded.

x Should your company go public, anticipate a loss in decision-making flexibility too. Your compensation will be critically scrutinized; and opportunities that come your way may, of necessity, become corporate opportunities, opportunities that may well be lost since outside directors and even shareholders may need to approve a decision before the company can act.

x Officers and directors of publicly held corporations are subject to increasing personal liability—for self-dealing and other conflicts of interest, for failure to exercise "due diligence," for negligence. And indemnification or insurance cannot fully cover this exposure.

x The management of a publicly held company may be preoccupied with the consequences of their decisions on the day-to-day market price of corporate stock. So, an R&D program may be wrongly scrapped, since it reduces short-term profits, even though it may boost long-term growth.

x For the sake of public appeal, a public company may pay dividends to its shareholders—taxable to you at up to 70 percent—while now, as a privately held business under your exclusive control, dividends are being kept to a minimum or avoided altogether.

x In its ultimate valuation of your public stock for estate-tax purposes, the IRS will consider its market price. The result: certainly a higher valuation than would apply to the same stock were the business privately owned.

11•10
WHAT DO YOU HAVE TO OFFER?

In weighing the positives against the negatives, evaluate yourself too. Your eligibility for public financing will depend on your sales and earnings (as compared with industry trends), the adequacy of your current and projected working capital and cash flow levels, the quality of your management, and the future your business faces. As soon as you conclude that going public is the next logical step for your business, seek help. With the counsel of your lawyer, your accountant, and your banker, find the best managing underwriter you can.

Once selected, your underwriter may form a syndicate, commit to purchase all the securities you offer, and then resell what he can to the general public. Or, more commonly, he may act as your agent and use his best efforts to sell your offering to the general public for a fee of 7 to 10 percent of the proceeds.

First, though, your underwriter will advise and assist you in engineering the most intense metamorphosis your business will ever undergo.

⇒ *The preliminaries.* Going public will be preceded by months of internal preparation, including a corporate reorganization (and often a recapitalization), a restructuring of titles to real estate, a rearrangement of permitted insiders' agreements (including stock option and other privileges), a rewriting of the corporate charter and bylaws and a general revamping of most financial arrangements.

These, of course, presume the give-and-take decisions about the type, number, and price of securities to be sold. Usually, at least 200,000 common shares are offered at $5 each, wisely underpriced to assure a favorable aftermarket.

⇒ *The registration.* The Securities Act of 1933 requires any company making a public offering to disclose accurately and fully all pertinent information about the company and its offering. Athough the SEC, the Act's enforcer, demands comprehensive disclosure, it will not pass judgment on the merits of the company or the security. Compliance with the Act requires the filing of a two-part registration statement consisting of the prospectus and "supplementary information."

A prospectus is a disclosure document, designed to inform the Commission and any prospective buyer about the structure, history, finances and dealings of the company, and about the nature of the proposed offering in a literal, formalized manner. At the same time, the prospectus serves as an advertising document to induce offerees to buy. And so a balance must be struck between conservatism and optimism. The product must neither misrepresent nor mislead, and conservatism must triumph—even to the point of highlighting adverse factors including operating losses, dependence on key suppliers or customers, conflicts of interest, and increasing industry regulation.

Supplementary information includes financial statements and detailed information about past offerings in a question-and-answer format. Supplementary information is not distributed publicly, but it is open for public inspection at the Commission's offices and thus is available to sophisticated investors.

A footnote: Regulation A allows a short-form, "baby" registration for self-underwriters of offerings not exceeding $500,000 (or smaller professionally underwritten offerings). Not only does Regulation A provide a simpler and cheaper way to go public, it may be quicker: "baby" registrations are filed at easily accessible regional SEC offices.

⇒ *The waiting period.* After the registration statement is filed, expect to wait several months until it becomes effective. In the interim, the Commission will review your statement and may issue a letter of comment (or a deficiency letter), seeking more facts or a revision in your prospectus. During your statement's pendency, securities may not be sold, but they may be described in "tombstone" ads, word-of-mouth pitches and preliminary prospectus ("red herring") mailings. "Indications of interest" may be accepted from would-be buyers, but actual sales may not yet be consummated, nor may offers to buy or sell be issued.

⇒ *The effective date.* Congratulations! You are now free to sell your securities. And you are now bound to disclose publicly and promptly all material developments—good or bad—that might affect the value of your securities. You are obliged to refrain from trading on inside information until it is publicly disclosed. And you are prohibited from selling your controlling shares except in the manner and to the extent the law will allow. Should your publicly held company have assets in excess of $1 million and more than 500 shareholders (or should its stock be listed on a stock exchange), you will be subject to the additional registration requirements of the Securities Act of 1934. These include annual (form 10K), quarterly (form 10Q) and special (form 8K) disclosures (which are also required of 300-shareholder companies whose securities are registered under the 1933 Act); special rules relating to the solicitation of proxies, insider reporting, and accountability for short-term profits by directors, officers and 10 percent shareholders; and tender-offer reporting.

11•11
SUCCESS AT LAST

A well-planned public offering must result from a long-range study under the guidance of your attorney, who will eventually recruit the brainpower of a top-flight securities attorney. Yet going public is not always a necessary move in the growth of a profitable business, nor, as we have seen, is it always wise. Entertaining a public offering and its alternatives is merely one sign that you have achieved a measure of success and fulfillment that others may rightfully envy.

INDEX